VIETNAM ABYSS

A JOURNAL OF UNMERITED GRACE

MICHAEL J. SNOOK

WITH STAN CORVIN, JR.
AUTHOR OF *VIETNAM SAGA*

SOUTHWESTERN
LEGACY PRESS

Annette,

Hope you enjoy reading Vietnam Abyss. I will Look forward to seeing you in AA meetings, one day at a time. God Bless Michael J. Snook

11-06-2018

PUBLISHER'S NOTE

"Trigger Warning"

Please note that *Vietnam Abyss: A Journal of Unmerited Grace* contains graphic, written descriptions of a Vietnam veteran who suffered from severe Post-Traumatic Stress Disorder (PTSD), mental illness and alcoholism. Some readers may find parts of the book disturbing, and which may "trigger" their own strong feelings regarding some issues described. However, through intense counseling, treatment and his participation in an alcohol rehab program the author Michael J. Snook ultimately recovered from his PTSD, insanity and overcame his alcoholism. Hopefully, this story will offer some encouragement and healing to the reader.

Southwestern Legacy Press, LLC

Design Services: Melinda Martin, MartinPublishingServices.com

PUBLISHING INFORMATION:
ICB - Scripture is taken from the International Children's Bible®. Copyright © 1986, 1988, 1999 by Thomas Nelson All rights reserved.
NLT - New Living Translation, copyright © 1996, 2004, 2007 by Tyndale House Foundation. All rights reserved.
NKJV - Scripture is taken from the New King James Version®. Copyright © 1982 by Thomas Nelson. All rights reserved.
NIV - Scripture quotations marked (NIV) are taken from the Holy Bible, New International Version®, and NIV®. Copyright © 1973, 1978, 1984, 2011 by Biblica, Inc. ™ Used by permission of Zondervan. All rights reserved worldwide. The "NIV" and "New International Version" are trademarks registered in the United States Patent and Trademark Office by Biblica, Inc. ™

ISBN: 978-1-7327625-3-4 Paperback
        978-1-7327625-1-0 Hardback
        978-1-7327625-2-7 eBook

PUBLISHED BY: Southwestern Legacy Press
        8901 Tehama Ridge Parkway
        Suite 127-115
        Fort Worth, TX 76177
        stan@swlegacypress.com

LIBRARY CATALOGING:
Names: Snook, Michael J. (Michael J. Snook)
Co-Author: Corvin, Jr. Stan (Stan Corvin, Jr.)
Vietnam Abyss: A Journal of Unmerited Grace
[190 pages] 23cm × 15cm (9in. × 6 in.)

Description: Vietnam Abyss is the inspiring true story of a Vietnam Veteran who descends into the darkness of chronic Post Traumatic Stress Disorder (PTSD), alcoholism, insanity and multiple confinements in a Veterans Administration psychiatric ward then later through his participation in PTSD counseling sessions and the program of Alcoholics Anonymous recovers and becomes a born-again Christian and certified minister.

Key Words: Vietnam War, Vietnam Tet of 1968, Saigon, Ho Chi Minh City, Long Binh, Bien Hoa, Post Traumatic Stress Disorder, PTSD, Mental Health, Agent Orange, Veterans Administration, VA, Alcoholics Anonymous, AA, Twelve-Step Recovery Program, Celebrate Recovery, Addiction.

TABLE OF CONTENTS

FOREWORD

On Memorial Day weekend in 2014, I met Michael after speaking at a church service, and he told me that he was a Vietnam veteran and could speak Vietnamese. We talked about the ministry I was doing thru my foundation, and I was impressed with his openness, sincerity, and enthusiasm for the Lord. I asked him to call Pastor Dan Dang in Fort Worth and arrange a visit to our offices. Michael and his wife Lori came to Texas and met everyone.

Six months later in March 2015, they both traveled with my staff and me to Vietnam to assist with our ministry there. Michael had not been back since his disastrous time while living there in 1998. The trip was a healing experience for him. In April of 2016, I asked Michael to join my staff in Fort Worth and assist us in our international Vietnamese ministry. He moved to Fort Worth and today continues to travel to Vietnam with the REAP mission team.

Someone once said, "When the world tells you to give up, Hope whispers, Try one more time." In many ways, that has been part of my life's mantra. For those of you unfamiliar with my story, in July of 1969, I was with the United States Navy serving as a riverboat gunner in Vietnam. During a firefight with NVA and Vietcong combatants, I was poised to throw a white phosphorous grenade when it exploded in my hand, and I was burned beyond recognition over most of my body. The ordeal hospitalized me for fourteen months where I underwent numerous surgeries. Since then I have had over fifty reconstruction operations. My survival and life are a miracle and a testimony of the resilience of the human spirit through the grace and mercy of Almighty God. Therefore, I am very familiar with the concept of perseverance and "grit" as we sometimes say in Texas.

Michael's book describes in graphic detail his downward spiral into the abyss of PTSD, alcoholism, insanity, and suicidal thoughts. However, it also tells of his subsequent remarkable road to recovery after an encounter with what can only described as an angel he met in a bar in Laos while on a trip up the Mekong River where he intended to commit suicide in the jungle.

Vietnam Abyss: A Journal of Unmerited Grace will be a beacon of light and hope in the life of anyone who is struggling with PTSD, addiction and mental illness. In conclusion, I want to say that Michael's Snook's book is a masterfully written and intriguing look into the life of a man who ultimately survives the Vietnam War and his own demons.

Dave Roever
September 2018

Blessed is the one who perseveres under trial
because, having stood the test, that person will
receive the crown of life that the Lord has promised
to those who love him.
—James 1:12 (NIV)

I
PREFACE

Saint Augustine (354-430 A.D.) wrote one of the first great Western autobiographies. He wrote about his immoral life as a lost person and subsequent conversion to Christianity. The title of his book was *Confessions*. The confession – redemption pattern remained the model for autobiographical writing for more than a thousand years.

The journal that you are about to read revives that model and is set in a modern-day tragedy that moves from spiritual darkness to a redeemed life of grace.

Eastern religion, philosophy, and martial arts had been an essential part of my life up to that point and sustained me fairly well. My bookshelves were packed full of self-help books. However, now I no longer search for meaning in those books. Meaning is all around us. My path included studying those books, my chronic alcoholism, and the practicing of martial arts. Most of my searching was complicated and strenuous work. None of that effort brought the answers I so desperately needed. If I were to suggest a simpler more direct way, I would say, "Just give up; quit trying so hard, quit fighting. Just sit down, shut up and listen." A friend of mine who has thirty-two years of sobriety puts it this way, "Don't just do something, sit there." In July 1975, I began a new journey. My contact with reality began the day I quit placing alcohol in my body. Except for two relapses, I have not returned to that personal delusion. The body must be free of mood-altering chemicals before the mind can begin to function properly.

After a few sober years, my thinker started to work again. Then I realized that physically I was a wreck, so I became involved in the martial arts. With a clear mind and a healthier body, I started to experience life. I still sought methods of escape, but my methods were less harmful to others and myself.

In the beginning, I placed reliance on people. This worked for a while but then the people left, because, after all, people are material objects too. Finally, I was told to place my reliance on God, but I could not find Him. Then friends in my Alcoholics Anonymous (AA) group suggested that I "act as if" I believed in God. They suggested that I spend ten minutes every morning on my knees praying to God, even if I did not believe in Him. They also suggested that I quit asking for things and even told me what I could say in a simple prayer like, "Thy will, not mine be done," or a little longer one like the Serenity Prayer.

"God grant me the serenity to accept the things I cannot change. The courage to change the things I can and the wisdom to know the difference."

It took several years before I could find the humility to kneel, even in private. At first, it was only on one knee alone in the bathroom. It seemed like a noble thing to do, one knee, like the Knights of the Round Table.

Please understand that none of what I have is a result of anything I have done. My way led to death and destruction for others and myself. Each day I live is another gift. For me to really live, I had to quit running the show. What I have found is a new freedom. Today I have the profound belief that everything will be all right.

My faith is grounded in the present. All we have is this day, but what an opportunity it is. My daily life is contingent on my spiritual condition. I know that my life is an extremely fragile thing. All of this can be taken away in a few minutes.

Here are some of the things I was told to do. I try to stay in the present moment most of the time, accept responsibility for my behavior, do not keep any secrets, say please in the morning and thank you at night, refrain from using the word "I" too often, and practice "To thine own self be true."

The journal that follows is copied from two separate ones that were hand written by me. The first was written from 1996 to 1998. It is the tragic story of my life as a guilt-ridden Vietnam veteran where I lost everything because of my separation and divorce, tearing apart my family and ending my twenty-six-year marriage.

The divorce also aggravates my Post Traumatic Stress Disorder (PTSD) resulting in three confinements in the VA psychiatric ward, the loss of eighteen years of sobriety, several near death suicide attempts, and a two-year relapse into the spiritual darkness that eventually takes me back to Vietnam. Subconsciously, I believe I returned there to die.

The road back from darkness and insanity is a long road that leads me to Gods unmerited grace and a new life. It is a story set down in part by my writings in a God journal written ten years later in 2006-08. The divine intervention took place much earlier while in Vietnam in 1998. It included the appearance of an angel, in the person of a female Peace Corps Worker, who I believe was sent by God to Vientiane, Laos to retrieve me from a suicide trip. What followed was one more confinement in a Veterans Administration's psychiatric ward and then the gradual rebuilding of a life.

After a yearlong battle with the demons of alcoholism and the constant craving for a drink, I had one last binge drunk. The next morning I was finally ready to get on my knees before the God of my youth and ask for forgiveness and help. This turning point took place on June 11, 2000. That surrender brought about a new life with God's unmerited grace and mercy as its foundation, and I am eternally grateful.

Michael J. Snook
September 1, 2018

II
SPIRITUAL DESTRUCTION OF
A VIETNAM VETERAN

Monday, April 14, 1996

I lost my last year's journal. I must have left it on the road some-where. Anyway, a lot happened in 1995. I sold a house, bought another house, moved to a different job, we moved to Las Vegas, and Mom died. But, today I am sitting in the Red Roof Inn in Naperville, IL. I am taking advanced intelligent network training tomorrow. It has been a very frustrating day today. My largest cus-tomer is starting to back out of a $4.2 million central office terminal contract.

Today is my third day without eating any flesh. I had spaghetti with tomato sauce tonight. I feel tired and lost tonight. I have been feeling lonely and separated a lot lately. I am not sure why.

Next week Donna and I will have been married twenty-five years. It has been twenty-five good years. Also, I will turn forty-nine years old next week. It is cloudy and cold here today. I prefer that the sun shine every day as it does at home in Las Vegas.

I am feeling sad. It seems like nobody knows where I am right now. It seems like nobody knows and nobody cares. I guess I will call home, talk to my friend, and mate Donna. God Bless this year and my family.

****

Several years ago, I lived in an old three-story house in Minneapolis, Minnesota. In the attic of this old house was a study packed full of ancient books. Donna and our four children lived downstairs, while I spent most of my life in the attic with my books.

I had tacked index cards on the walls around my desk. On those cards were listed profound statements about life written by famous people since the beginning of time.

One evening after dinner I slipped up to my study, opened the book I had been reading, *The Secret Doctrine* by Madame Blavatsky, and found a white index card where my bookmark had been. It said, "Reading about life is fine, as long as you don't forget how to live it." Signed, Your Wife.

Donna was right. Something snapped in my mind. I realized that I had been searching for life in books and in the process had missed it. Hopefully, this paper will say something about my reality as I currently understand it.

My interest in Oriental religions can be traced to the two years I spent in the US Army stationed in Vietnam. In 1967, 1968, and 1969, I was introduced to the Oriental culture, language, and belief system. I visited Hong Kong and Japan during those years and became interested in the martial arts.

While in Vietnam, I learned to speak and write Vietnamese. I later studied Mandarin Chinese at the University of Minnesota and just completed my second year of Chinese at the University of Missouri, Kansas City. I have studied Tae Kwon Do (A Korean Martial Art) since 1976 and spent many years as a Black Belt instructor in that style.

My motive for writing this is that I seek personal clarification of how I have become the person I am today and what personal beliefs sustain me.

INTO THE ABYSS

*How long must this go on? How long must I see
war and death surrounding me?*

—Jeremiah 4:21 (TLB)

Wednesday, May 1, 1996

Today I am at the Westin hotel in Houston Texas. I have been here since this past Monday. I am feeling tired tonight. I went to an AA meeting earlier. I was supposed to go to the Astrodome for some stupid game, but I went to an AA meeting instead. I guess I prefer it that way. I have been sober since August 14, 1978. That is almost eighteen years.

My job is as crazy as ever. I keep running day and night. I have been traveling a lot. This morning, though, I was on my knees asking God to keep me clean and sober. Surrendering my life to God has been working well so far.

Last week Donna and I celebrated twenty-five years of marriage, and I turned forty-nine years old. Life has been very good to me. We have $95k in savings for retirement. I have stayed sober through the death of my mother, my prostate cancer, multiple moves, and lost jobs. Today life is good, but it seems like "pain has been the touchstone of my spiritual growth" over the years.

Happiness is like a butterfly if you run and chase it, it is very elusive; but if you sit quietly on a park bench, it may come and light on your shoulder.

Sunday, May 19, 1996

It is 9:31 pm in my little hotel room in Hickory Ridge Lisle, IL. I have been here for five days of company training. It took me three hours to get here on the plane. I hate flying into O'Hare airport.

However, once I got here, I found they have great vegetarian food and a fitness center that is nice. I need to whip myself into shape. It has been one week and two days with no meat, candy, pop, or caffeine. I have lost about ten pounds on this low-fat diet. I cannot believe I was up to 208 pounds. When I left the hospital after cancer surgery in 1993, I weighed 165 pounds. I have been getting fatter ever since. I must start to turn that around.

I want to spend some time on the activities of my life this week also. I need to get my life on a piece of paper and begin to prioritize my actions. Work seems to take too much of my mental and physical time. I have applied for three different jobs. One of the positions is in Tianjin China, and the other two would be working as a sales manager. All three jobs are realistic opportunities. I have an interview this Friday about the China job. I have been studying Mandarin just waiting for an opportunity like this one.

I have been spending some time in exercise and Buddhism recently too. I am still seeing the Burmese monk. I guess I am still trying to move toward perfection.

Smooth flat rock found
in Delmar, on public phone
booth.
Old hag with rags on her head
Wishes she was dead.
Eat no more flesh. Eat only fruit
and vegetables with beans
and rice (steamed white rice from
Thailand).
Drink no more pop, coffee, or
alcohol, drink only fresh fruit
juice and water.
This is good enough for you.
You be very healthy now.
For you do not wear fancy
clothes or gold rings. Dress
simple. Wear life like loose
rags.
For you to sleep on soft bed is
no good. You sleep on floor
is much better.
For you drive car very unhealthy.
Walk much better.
You worry too much. Just forget
about it. Job, money, no big
deal. For you can be okay with nothing.

Monday, June 17, 1996

I am once more back in Lisle for another training update. My life is good today because it has been five weeks without eating any flesh. I have lost twenty-three pounds, and I feel wonderful. I have been working out every day for three weeks. It has been mostly running and lifting weights. I have increased my sitting and walking meditation time too. Yesterday was Father's Day. The kids got me another meditation cushion to sit on. Jay at AA always says, "Feel good. Aint hung over today."

I did not get the China job. Things are going well in Vegas. I guess I will stay there a while longer. We are going to Minnesota for July 4th. That should be a fun time.

This journal lacks something. I think it may be a lack of philosophical delusion.

Such as:

- Nothing belongs to us.
- Even this sack of flesh and bones is very temporary.
- The ego will die soon.
- Death is certain!
- The body dies no matter what you eat, drink, or smoke.
- No matter how physically, spiritually or mentally fit you are, death will take you soon.
- Who are you now?
- Who will you be after the flesh starts to decay?

Sunday, July 14, 1996

I just got off the phone with my brother in Orlando Florida. He is a good man. He is one of maybe two men that can be trusted. I bought forty acres of woods west of Henning, MN for $23k. I also bought two AK-47's and five hundred rounds of ammo the other day. We had a nice vacation in Minnesota. My brother Sonny took the week off, and we had a good time fishing and hanging out together.

I saw John and Emily last night. They were in town for a while.

Monday, July 15, 1996

It is another week in this life. Donna started a new job this morning at 6:00 am. She is working as an office assistant for a local company.

Yesterday the history channel had a special about the CIA in Vietnam. It was about the Phoenix Program. It brought back memories from the past that I have not thought about in many years. The CIA interviewed me when I got home from Vietnam. They sent a letter to my uncle's house in Seattle. When I met with them, I told them that I wanted to spend a year in Monterey, California for intensive Vietnamese language training and then to be sent back to Vietnam. They told me they could not make any promises on what job I would get after finishing my training in Langley, so I declined their offer.

VIETNAM FLASHBACKS

Tuesday, July 16, 1996

This morning I started writing down some Vietnam memories that I have been having recently. It is difficult writing about the thoughts that flood my mind. One night during the 1968 Tet Offensive, I left the bunker after waking up the other guard. My memory was blank until I remembered that later all hell broke loose around our bunker. We began taking fire from both rocket-propelled grenades (RPG's) and small arms. My memories are still very vague. I do remember that we later confirmed that a man who crawled through the nearby concertina wire was a hard-core NVA soldier and was testing our perimeter before the main attack on our radio relay station.

The second incident happened when I was in Bien Hoa several weeks after Tet had started. I just flashed back to when a Vietcong soldier, with a machete, tried to kill me in a Chinese movie theater. I remember he chased me outside into a dark alley. At that point, my memory is blank; however, somehow I was able to escape and return to my unit. Some other things I remembered while sitting at my desk this morning:

1.   The person that hung himself from the water tower next to our hooch and because of a "Dear John Letter" was a good friend of mine.

2.   I witnessed a bomb blast at a bar in Bien Hoa where several GIs died.

3.   I remembered that someone fragged a second lieutenant in our company. They tied a string to his hooch door and the other end to the pin of a grenade. I do not remember if he died or not.

I have always known that I probably killed the enemy during nighttime firefights, but until today, I could not believe that I killed people. I have started getting therapy at the Veterans Administration (VA) again to work through these memories.

I know that under my skin I became Vietnamese to survive in Vietnam. If I became the enemy, I could not hate him without hating myself or kill him without killing myself. My idealism covered the truth. The truth was that I was like many of the GIs. I too had a breaking point. I too had a point where I lost my sanity. When the rain, heat, and bugs got to me, I cracked. I have always maintained that I was different from the others. I was stronger. I could adapt. I would not go crazy. I would survive no matter what the cost. They would not break me. Two years twelve days in hell and I could have taken more. I hated myself for years after Nam because I had become just like the Vietcong. I was ruthless. My self-loathing was overwhelming.

My neck aches I must stop writing now. Dr. Nancy said this would be like opening a pus sore. It must only be done a little at a time, and I will do it without the VA's medications. The medications will lead me to drink alcohol, and that will kill me.

Monday, July 22, 1996

I just remembered the reoccurring nightmare. I slipped out under the perimeter wire past the bunkers. I would go into the villages and crawl from hooch to hooch looking for something. I could never find what I was looking for and would wake up screaming with the night sweats.

Last week I realized what I might have been looking for. I was looking in those Vietnamese huts for myself. I was looking for the young kid that entered the war at Bien Hoa Air Force base on July 7, 1967.

An Omaha VA shrink, once told me that I had become Vietnamese under my skin. When I departed Vietnam, I left my youth, my innocence, my ability to love, my ability to feel, and my soul. Many young men died in Vietnam. Some of us survived as only empty shells of our former selves. A few of us came home as the walking dead.

Twenty-five years with the loving support of a good woman and eighteen years of sobriety are the only reason I have any sanity left. Thank you, Mr. VA, for the rest.

Friday, July 26, 1996

I am sitting in a hotel in Kansas City. I had lunch with my son and daughter a little while ago, and now I am ready to get back to Vegas. I am feeling worn out and ready to get back in the sunlight. I find cloudy days depressing.

I have been thinking about the forty acres of land in Minnesota. I am not sure what I want to build on it. I know I want to pay off the loan before anything else. We have several options after the land is paid off.

They include:

1. Use a small two-wheel trailer for the next six years until I retire.
2. Build a 988 sq. ft. cabin out of logs.
3. Build a large cabin with walk out basement and a wraparound deck.

Pros and Cons:

- Option one: Cheap $4k, functional, not secure, not what I want, vandals, temporary.
- Option two: Expensive $35k, functional, looks good, secure, could build it myself, permanent.
- Options three: $85k very expensive, will not use much next six years, lots of space, Looks great, vandals might be a problem I don't need year around.

Reasons for the land: I want a place of my own that is free of debt. It is a summer home that we can use to get away from the Las Vegas heat. Will always be a summer only home. It is a place to rest and eventually die and be buried. Place me in a wooden casket with no embalming fluid, please.

Monday, August 5, 1996

I am in Hood River, Oregon today visiting customers. I will be in Nebraska next week and Minnesota the following week. This job is fun, fun, and more fun. Last Friday my youngest daughter and I went to Laguna Beach. We had a great time swimming. We rode the big roller coaster at the state line. The plan was to ride it again on the way back home, but we were both too afraid to get back on for a second ride. I enjoyed the two days with her. One of my few regrets is that I did not spend more time with the kids after they turned thirteen. It seems like I got in the way of that and the travel now makes it even more difficult.

I have been acting strange lately. I am giving Donna little digs. I guess I am feeling insecure about her working in a warehouse with a bunch of men. Also, I miss having her home in the mornings and afternoons. I do not know what I would do if we ever had a serious fight. It has been many years since any major disputes. I worry about our relationship. I could deal with changes in job or health, but I do not think I could handle not being with my wife. I love her a lot, I guess. I had better give her a call.

Saturday, August 10, 1996

I was meeting with Dr. Nancy at the VA yesterday morning and had a major panic attack that led to a flashback outside in the car. Dr. Nancy and I were talking in her office when she was called out for a minute. I sat there and suddenly, I started sweating and hyperventilating. It was so bad I got up and ran out of the building. When I got to my car, I had the flashback. It was a terrifying experience:

I was in a bunker in the fetal position, and I could not breathe. I was hyperventilating and having muscle cramps. I had an overwhelming feeling of fear and panic. I had a loss of motor functions. My arms shook violently. Next thing I knew Dr. Nancy was in the car with me telling me to take deep breathes, hold them and relax my body.

Every time I go to the VA, I sweat and shake. It is difficult just to walk into a VA building. I am not sure why. What is most amazing to me about the flashback is that I was actually there. I could feel it escalating as if I would never be able to come back to reality. Dr. Nancy's calm voice was all that brought me back.

It seemed like there were three separate spaces. The bunker, my body, and my emotions were all three present in the flashback. The voice of Dr. Nancy was separate from where I was in the bunker. I could hear in the present, but there was another space or focus. There was a light leading me down a path that contained neither the past nor the present. It felt like it led to death. I guess that is what disassociation is all about.

Monday, August 12, 1996

I am still dealing with the aftermath of last Friday. I cannot understand how my body and mind can become damaged like that. I was not able to function, the shakes, hyperventilation, all that stuff. Now my concern is where it will go from here. I have had continued anxiety since Friday. I am very spacey and cannot seem to concentrate or focus. I still have the anti-anxiety drug that Dr. Nancy gave me, but I have not used any yet.

I am still full of fear. It is an almost paralyzing fear. I keep wondering if it escalated, would the dead bodies have been there. My mouth keeps drying up. I am having trouble swallowing. I must not think about it anymore. I must focus on being here right now. Everything is all right if I can only stay here, right here,

Wednesday, August 14, 1996

I do not know what happened to yesterday, but I think today is Wednesday. I received my eighteen-year sobriety chip from Jimmy A. over at my AA club this morning. It was good to see him. He was a Marine in Vietnam and has been a good friend of mine since 1984.

I am not sure what happened yesterday. I guess I spent the day in class. I must have had dinner alone again. I think I started taking the drugs today, but it may have been yesterday or maybe Monday night.

I certainly do not feel any anxiety since taking them. I am having a few minor side effects, for instance when I bend over I lose my balance. I also get some minor muscle twitching soon after taking a pill. The medicine is Lorazepam 1mg every four-six hours. It says on the bottle that it is supposed to make me drowsy. I did doze off in a couple of AA meetings, but that is not abnormal for me. I guess I should add that I spoke with Donna and Dr. Nancy on Monday night in a bit of frenzy because of the anxiety and flashbacks. They suggested that it is the medication, and it does seem to be working quite well. However, somehow I ended up here in Omaha.

I will say goodbye for now.

Thursday, August 15, 1969

How many days has it been now?

How long have we been running with the hounds snapping at our heels never daring to look back? The biggest fear is the fear of death of a sane mind. Nothing will ever be allowed to come between life, and the last breath-nothing is of greater importance, at least at this stage.

What do you want; death or perhaps you want to be betrayed by the one you love? I visited my sister Clare in the hospital again tonight. She is crazy. She said my wife had cheated on me with my best friend.

My life seems full of darkness and gloom tonight. I am tired now. I must sleep.

I am going to Minnesota tomorrow to buy the land.

Okay?

Wednesday, August 28, 1996

I do not know how to start this time. I just read the several past writings. Actually, I read through May. These past few months have been hell. I need to clarify what happened as best I can at this time. Please note that on August 15th, I thought it was still 1969.

I started getting ready for this back in May with the diet, weight loss, meditation, and exercise. Today, I am on the other side. I am not sure why, or how, but for now I have survived.

Recap:

Jul 15-29	Saw Dr. Nancy
Aug 9-27	Saw Dr. Nancy
Aug 9	Had flashback at her office
Aug 12	Took Ativan in Omaha because of shakes and fear in a hotel room.
Aug 14	Eighteen years sober.

Aug 15	Went to Vet center with Jimmy A.
Aug 16	Drove to Henning. Slept at Dan's and closed the deal on the land.
Aug 17	Sonny and I stayed at Dan's.
Aug 19	Spent last night at Sonny's still on Ativan been trying to cut back to one pill per day. Left to see Taft and ended up in Omaha about 1:30 am--- spent $100 at a Casino.
Aug 20	saw Jimmy A. and took the plane home.
Aug 20	Donna's birthday.
Aug 21	Home still on Ativan. I am really messed up. I'm becoming dependent on it but still trying to cut back.
Aug 22	Saw Dr. Nancy. She prescribed antidepressants and said I should start taking it in the morning and Ativan in the afternoon. Picked up Mark at the airport, picked up medication on the way home. Spoke to Jim at vet center and took last Ativan pill. Donna and I had a heated discussion about medication.

Aug 23	Went to work. Very little ability to focus. No medication.
Aug 24	Went to the AA men's stag meeting told them of my decision not to take the VA medication. I bought Donna a new car today.
Aug 25	Went to a movie with Donna and Mark.
Aug 26	Went to work. Threw away all medication and called Dr. Nancy's office to cancel all future appointments. Decided to do ninety-in-ninety meetings with AA. One day at a time.
Aug 27	Work and meetings. Feel okay.

That brings me to today, and I am still too close to see the past objectively. However, this is what I know today. I probably do have PTSD. I go through a cycle every year until August 14th which is my sobriety birthday and my mother's birthday.

1. I will not take the VA's meds.
2. I will not return there.
3. The answer is not in drugs.
4. I may never totally recover.
5. Awareness will help
6. The fear is real - and so are the flashbacks.

I am okay today. I still am not sure what is right - many have urged me toward the medication including my friend Corky H. I still feel the internal struggle going on. I feel more secure because of the AK-47's and Gerber knife that I bought recently.

Peace - I have written enough for today.

(EMDR) EYE MOVEMENT DESENSITIZATION REPROCESSING

Sunday, September 1, 1996

It is one more day in the life of this body. I saw Dr. Lois, a clinical psychologist, last Wednesday afternoon. She specializes in Post-Traumatic Stress Disorder (PTSD). We talked for an hour about what had happened at the VA. She said that Ativan is an incredibly addictive drug used for anxiety. She is very supportive of working through this thing without medication. Maybe I will not have to go through it again next year.

I feel like a completely different person from who I was a week ago. I went to the Saturday morning AA men's stag meeting. I had several supportive comments from the people about the change I have made since last Saturday.

Today I feel free from the fear and anxiety. I need to call Jimmy A. and see how he is doing. I have a lot going on with the job right now. I do not know if we will have any work left here next year. I guess it depends on pending contract bids.

I am tense about the kids and Donna with her working so

hard. But having said that, Praise God! I am clean and sober one more day. My old sponsor from Minneapolis Bob T. has Alzheimer's disease. I spoke to him the other day again. I am sorry to hear about his sickness because he is a good person.

Theresa and Lee called this past week. I spoke to Lee for a while. He sure is a good kid. Very bright like his dad Sonny and strong like his uncle. I'm sure his dad is as proud of him as I am.

Mark and I just finished cleaning the garage and yard. I enjoy having him back from Kansas City. I was worried about him staying there. Sons are special.

My sales numbers are better than the rest of the teams, but I need to hit 100% by September 31st to make an extra $15k. That would sure be nice.

"I can see clearly now; the rain is gone."

"There are no dark clouds overhead."

Praise God, bless Donna and Brother Chuck!

Saturday, September 7, 1996

It has been another week. I went to the therapist on Thursday. We talked about family and sadness. We did not speak about PTSD much. I guess, next Thursday we will start working on those issues. Donna is concerned about me going there. She has mixed feelings every time I seek help. She is especially leery since I used the VA's drugs.

A lot is going on with my job again. We do not know if we have the telecommunications product business for the next three years. I have been busy and stressed over it all. We bought $23k in land and $16k for a car in the past month, so finances are getting tight – even with Donna working. I need to get a couple of large bonus checks to pay off the car. The payments for the car do not start until October. Outside of that, everything is going pretty well. I am still active in AA on a daily basis.

Right now, I feel like I am in a lull between two storms the PTSD, VA, crazy person and the compulsive, obsessed, driven survivor. However, today, I know that I can go through either and survive. Maybe I can even let go of both and just be me.

"I know who I am, what I am, and where I am." That is per Corky.

Monday, September 9, 1996

I stayed home this week rather than go to Denver. I am trying to pull in all my sales before the end of the fiscal year, which is the end of this month. If I can make my 100% by the end of the sales year, (which is $10.6M more in sales) I will get an extra $15k bonus. I am pretty sure I can make it.

I had a busy day talking to customers and company people. I also found time to go to two AA meetings. AA is an integral part of my life, and I hope it always will be. Sometimes I feel sad about the busy life. There are not enough hours in a day to live this life to its fullest. However, if I slow down and reflect, that is uncomfortable too.

I have been thinking about the land lately. I sure like having a piece of earth that is ours. My friend Jimmy A. had surgery for bedsores last week. I called him yesterday. He seemed like he was in good spirits.

This week I need to start working on the violence issues of Vietnam with the counselor. What is amazing to me is that I do not know anything about it today. It is literally as if it never happened.

Yet, I know it did happen. What I just went through was real. But where would I begin? Every day is another dream of truth:

> Blood splattered from the headless dove.
> Drink chicken blood.
> Breathe in, breathe out.
> Unclench your fists.
> Relax your wrists and right shoulder blade.
> Know the truth about the fear.
> Tam Hiep Prison – dead people walking – can you still feel their pain?
> Relax your mind.
> Travel back through time.
> Remember the heat, the rain, the smell.
> Nuoc mam cooking on the stove.
> Put it on your rice.
> See the truth clearly.
> The truth will set you free from obsession.

Thursday, September 12, 1996

I just got back from another session with Dr. Lois. I signed a waiver to start a new therapy. The new treatment is called Eye Movement Desensitization Reprocessing (EMDR). The way it works is pretty amazing. We had our first session, and this is what happened:

I was shaking badly when we started, and Dr. Lois said, "I think we should wait until next week to start because I am going to be out of town this weekend and I would rather not be gone in case anything happens from the session." I told her, "I think we ought to get started now. I have waited long enough." So I switched chairs.

My anxiety level was very high. My body was trembling on both sides, and while sitting there, my thighs were slightly quivering.

She had me form a mental picture of our agreed safe place on the beautiful hill on the forty acres I own in Minnesota. She then had me assign a word to a low-stress job type thing. I picked bids – which are pending contracts that were due October 1st.

By this time, my body was shaking quite badly. She had me close my eyes, I pictured the hill, and my body calmed down. Then after I opened them, she started moving two fingers back and forth in front of my eyes. When I followed the movements, my body immediately relaxed after each time. I took a deep breath. However, a few seconds after the calming effect, my body started shaking again even worse. Once or twice, I was unable to stop the shaking and focus on the fingers.

When she changed the directions of her finger movements, my body immediately calmed. It seemed I had control over how long the relaxed body stayed that way, but it always started shaking again. Now my left shoulder was shaking violently. My stomach, face, and legs were twitching. I began stuttering and had trouble getting words out.

At one point, my breathing was hyperventilating, but I was able to come back because of the rapid movement of my eyes. Amazing stuff! I almost cried because of this awareness. I was very close to my pre-flashback state even though my arms started shaking. At one point, I recognized the shaking as repressed fear located in different parts of my body.

Wonderful stuff!

The session only lasted thirty minutes, but my body was stiff from the work. She had me picture the hill and went through a couple of Rapid Eye Movements (REM's) to come all the way back. My body was so stiff I could barely get up out of the chair.

I realized that I needed to leave as much of this in her office as possible. I know that I can do that. Some of the fear has already lifted. I feel warm in my stomach and feel like crying right now.

I am back at home sitting at my desk and feeling okay. I have a picture of the hill on my computer screen. I get a warm feeling when I look at the picture.

Friday, September 13, 1996

Last night I was exhausted, so I went to bed at 8:00 pm and was sleeping by 9:00 pm. I had several dreams that were quite vivid. I was ice fishing on thin ice with a group of men. Later I was with some customers in a large old building that was leaking water, and the roof was caving in. Also, I was hanging from a fence. I had jumped over it into a very deep pit with water at the bottom. At the last minute, I grabbed hold of the chicken wire, and I was just hanging there. I could not let go or climb back up. It was strange that I did not have any strong emotional response to the dreams I just woke up and would fall back to sleep.

Monday, September 16, 1996

I am feeling very anxious today about this stupid job. I feel like it's all going down the tubes in Kansas City. There is a big meeting this afternoon with the upper management. My customers believe we may have upset enough of their executives that they do not want to do business with us going forward.

I went golfing with my customer Brian, last Friday. He told me our no longer supplying Hybrid Fiber Coax (HFC) product might be the bombshell that costs us all of their business.

The truth is that the decisions are being made in Kansas and there is not much I can do about it.

Thursday, September 19, 1996

I am going to see Dr. Lois again this morning, and I think I will take the rest of the week off work. It is strange that I feel okay right now and I had a good week.

Later the same day;

About one hour ago, I finished another session with Dr. Lois. It was an hour and a half session. Some weird stuff happened. I met at least a couple of sides of my personality. It is hard to write about it right now. Maybe I can try later. It seems like some assimilation needs to take place before I can get it on paper.

I am at home in our bed, and I feel okay. I am a little weak physically but okay. I am exhausted too... emotionally tired. I am going to take a long weekend. I need it.

Friday, September 20, 1996

I spent yesterday afternoon hiking up in Mt. Charleston with Mark. We had a great time. It is so quiet up there compared to here in the Vegas Valley. We ate shelled peanuts, walked and talked. We went to Robbers Roost Cave near the summit.

I later went to a meeting and spent the balance of the evening discussing my PTSD with Donna. I believe she thinks it is mostly crap and she is probably right. For sure, it is another period of our time together where I'm demanding attention and focus on myself. I need to try to see it from her perspective.

Now, let me set down as best I can what happened yesterday morning at Dr. Lois's office. To set the record straight, I bought a book on Neuro-Linguistic Programming (NLP) this week. It is called *Reframing* by Bandler. He writes about disassociation and parts that make up a personality. He believes that recovery happens when conflicting parts of personality can negotiate and see value in each other. To simplify it is the reunification of self. I am only about halfway through the book, so I am sure there will be other discoveries. I also ordered the $45.00 book on *EMDR* by Francine Shapiro.

With that rather lengthy preface, here is what happened yesterday morning during an hour and a half session with the doctor. I will write it down as my limited recall can remember it. I had a cup of tea and sat in the safe chair. Dr. Lois sat in her work chair. After drinking some tea and relating my rather common week, I moved to the chair near her where we do the work.

Soon after moving, she asked me to pick a scene or group of scenes. I first picked the Tet 1968 incident at the theater in Bien Hoa. She suggested combining the two. I closed my eyes, dropped both scenes, and instead selected the bunker scene that appeared during my flashback at the VA. We continued to talk about somewhat general things when suddenly I started getting jolts to my left side. They were like electric shocks. They were located low near my stomach.

Soon I was in a full shock state getting what felt like punches to my stomach, lower back, and thighs. She did the finger movements that would give me some relief; however, the physical reactions would immediately increase afterward. Pictures of the scene were being relived in my mind.

We had not established a clear safe place on the hill this time. A safe visual picture is required in conjunction with finger movements. I am having trouble writing about this right now. Anyway, I became aware of this presence or this separate part of myself. This other person was located on the left side of my body, and he had tremendous power and physical strength. He screamed, "My name is Bac Viet!"

He was strong, disciplined, and fearless. I had known him before; a long time ago. He was the one who was able to summon the strength to move my body when it was utterly paralyzed with fear in the bunker. During the session, my legs completely gave way, and they began thrashing about like jelly. I even cried out, "My legs won't move!" I am having trouble writing about what happened during the session.

My palms are sweating now as I try to write. What started the processing was after the jolts began I heard this voice say loud and clear, "It don't mean nothing." It said it several times, and my body would quit shaking or convulsing. I repeated what he said to me aloud. Later a softer side of me said, "My name is Michael, and it does mean something." It felt like I was claiming my internal house and it felt good to do that.

Soon after Bac Viet spoke, I got a flashback where I saw a Vietcong soldier behind a planter in the office. One side of me was strong and fighting the VC while the other side cowered and curled up in my chair. I would flop from one side of my chair to the other depending on which side of my personality was speaking.

After one side of my personality called the other side a coward, Dr. Lois asked, "Would you call your son Mark a coward?" What was weird was the Bac Viet side said, "Yes" while the Michael side said, "No." The Bac Viet side was very loud and forceful. He yelled, "Weak people die!" The phrase that kept coming up was, "I can hack it." I later remembered that that was how we pulled ourselves together emotionally during combat.

It felt as if during the session that conflict had control most of the time. There was this constant back and forth struggle. It seemed that the session, and my mind, was totally out of control.

The only other significant occurrence was that my body would crouch low in the right side of my chair. At first, it felt like a secure area in that part of the chair, but I soon experienced physical shocks there as well.

Dr. Lois said, "Everything that happened was normal. I have been through sessions where this type of physical movement also happens."

She said, "You did a tremendous amount of work yesterday and may have gotten through the worst of it."

I thought, "That would be good." I told her, "We need to define the safe place as my Minnesota hill next session."

I said, "I am having a great deal of difficulty writing about all this and assimilating it."

She replied, "You made a statement during the session that you could feel the stuff breaking up and, in fact, felt a piece of it leave your chest area."

She said, "This was significant because that is what will happen. It is like a bad chest cold; it will be coughed out in pieces until all the garbage is gone."

I must trust the process.

It is a beautiful fall day. I am going to enjoy it.

Saturday, September 21, 1996

I can see clearly; now the rain is gone. Looking back over the past two days, I am still not clear what transpired. Nevertheless, I feel more "together" right now, than I have in a long time.

Bandler says in his book, *Reframing, that* the different parts can talk to each other and do most of the time. The NLP process seems to allow conflict resolution between the elements and sees value in all components.

Three things have happened since the session. First, I just took two wonderful days off and did not work in my office. That is new.

Second, when I stood up for myself during the session and said, "My name is Michael, and it does mean something." I took ownership. I recognized the value in the Bac Viet side of my personality but realized his behavior was not appropriate at this time and in this place.

I said aloud during the session, "Even though the other side has tremendous strength, the middle personality part is stronger and smarter. After all, we have stayed alive, sober, and functioning extremely well since coming home from Vietnam."

Since that session, I have been able to express anger and stick up for myself several times. Tom called and asked how I was doing. I said, "I am doing fine even though you and Corky don't seem to agree."

Tom shuffled a bit, and I said, "Tom you need to know that Corky told me you suggested he call me a few weeks ago. He called and urged me to take the VA medications. I was at an extremely vulnerable place, and I have very high regard for you and Corky's opinion, but I am not going to take any more of the VA's drugs." Thank God!

I also got upset with the kids when they were having a battle during my conversation with Tom. And, I told Donna not to minimize my time in Vietnam. Perhaps I am somewhat sensitive right now.

I have had a few good days. I have been sleeping from 9:00 pm - 7:30 am. I am eating less and feeling better. Maybe I am over the hump. Stress level has dropped dramatically. The stress rashes on my right thigh and buttocks are almost entirely gone.

I went to the AA men's stag and talked a little about EMDR. I still do not know how long the process will take. I have had very little trauma during the week. EMDR is strange stuff that is for sure.

Tuesday, September 24, 1996

Yesterday I got a copy of Shapiro's book, *EMDR*. I spent about three hours reading it last night. He has an interesting therapeutic technique. I think that Dr. Lois is following his outline pretty well. I am somewhat concerned about the abreactions (physical contortions). I think my experience was quite close to a mental disassociation.

I have been feeling good since my last session. I guess balanced would be the right word. I am having anger outbursts that seem a little excessive, but I can work through them.

Yesterday the trash man got here, and Mark was still sleeping on the couch. I had yelled at him earlier about getting the trash out. I shouted even louder when I found him still sleeping at 1:00 pm. (I tried to carry some out and missed the truck so I was pissed at myself too.) Oh well, they will be here again Thursday.

The rashes are still gone even though I have the stress of my manager coming out from Kansas City to visit for the week. We will have dinner tonight and golf tomorrow.

Everything feels right today. I am relaxed and at ease with myself finally.

Sunday, September 29, 1996

It has been a quiet Sunday. We did not do much in last Thursday's session. We had only an hour session, so we did not do any EMDR. I am finding a need to go to a lot of AA meetings. I am still getting angry and coming off sideways at people.

My boss was here this week, and I snapped at him a few times. I thought I was supposed to take him to the airport at 8:30 am. I was early, and he did not get downstairs until 8:45. I was raging by the time he got there. He said, "Michael is there any possibility you could be wrong about what time I asked you to meet me?"

I said, "Absolutely not! I don't make mistakes when it comes to time." However, looking back on it maybe I was wrong. In fact, I was wrong after I checked my day timer notes.

I found a book called, *One Day at a Time* by Christy Lane. In the book, she writes about her trip to Vietnam. She said that Long Binh was overrun during the Tet offensive of 1969. Several hundred lost their lives that day. I do not recall the base was ever overrun, but maybe it was. I was located at a radio relay station a short distance north of the base.

I might make my sales number. I will be very close. I had better make the number because we need the extra cash. Donna is working overtime on her job today. I hate the fact that she has to be working.

Monday, September 30, 1997

I am continuing to have anger at the people around me. I snapped at the kids again today. Martha has been telling Donna that I seem angry a lot lately. Some of the anger is because I cannot seem to remember what it is that I am so angry about. It seems like I am being blocked from remembering my dreams or Vietnam memories about combat.

Last night Donna and I had a little spat in bed about how absorbed I am with this stuff. I snapped back at her. After our argument, I again had the intrusive image of the gun to my temple several times and heard the inner voice say, "You are going to kill yourself."

I used to have a voice that said, "Are we all going to die?" Dr. K., in Omaha, answered that for me when he said, "Yes, we are all going to die." For me, the question was simply, "Are we all going to die in this damn bunker!"

My hands get sweaty writing about these things. I cannot remember the incident where the VC soldier was behind the bush. I only remember the fear, panic and the inability to make my legs run. However, this I know, the subconscious remembers it all, and it will reprocess it if I allow it too.

I need to add two things to my September 20th writing. First, while I was in the fetal position in my chair, I was slowly reaching my hand out for help. I think I did this twice.

The second thing happened near the end of the physical reaction. While in my secure position in the chair, I began to laugh and asked Dr. Lois if she understood what was going on. I said, "I feel schizophrenic." She smiled and said, "You do not have schizophrenia you have PTSD." That was good to hear at the time. I continued to laugh, so I pulled myself up into an upright sitting position. Both of these things were strange but seemed like significant occurrences.

Perhaps this was indicative of closure on that fear scene. I guess we will find out the week after next when I go to my next session.

Monday, September 30, 1996

Wow, it sure has been a rough day. I am not sure where it started going wrong. Maybe it was the drunk at the noon AA meeting that had the dry heaves. He and I went out back during the meeting; I stood with him as he was vomiting and gave him my bottle of water to ease the pain. Then unexpectedly he said he was a Vietnam Vet and reached in his pocket and showed me his blue VA card with 40% disability typed on it. Chuck was his name. He was in bad shape. He had not eaten in several days.

I spent another two hours after the meeting talking to a different fellow. He said he had spent six months at rehab for PTSD. Some of the stuff he said twisted my mind for the rest of the day. I felt a lot of stress in my shoulders. He told me that he had blocked out 90% of the trauma that happened to him in Vietnam. Everything I told him about myself he kept saying, "Classic PTSD."

He told me to get rid of the ammo and guns, or I would end up killing myself. (I had Mark unload the AK's when I got home.)

Tonight I am fearful of what the future holds. I know for sure I will not die or take the easy way out by killing myself.

Praise God and Brother Chuck!

Wednesday, October 2, 1996

I am feeling much better today. I decided to place my life and will into God's hands early this morning. I even went to a 7:00 am AA meeting. I know that everything is going to be all right if I can just rely on God.

I spoke with Jimmy A. yesterday. Sometimes I get depressed when we talk. I think veterans can unintentionally feed each other's sickness.

Jimmy, Tim, Corky, Mike, Doc, George, all these guys care about me, but sometimes I just need to leave this PTSD stuff alone. I am not going off the deep end. And will not accept any such talk. My problem is that I buy into it and, in fact, seek out the conversations. However, it is not healthy for me to dwell on it right now.

I am going to Kansas City next week for work.

This pen sucks!

Saturday, October 5, 1996

I just got home from the men's stag meeting and breakfast. What a group. This morning I had Scott sitting next to me yelling about one of his customers. The continual noise got to me. Sometimes I am so full of fear in that room. Especially when it gets very loud like it did this morning. When I have that kind of fear, I want to strike out and hit the person. Stop the violence, stop the noise. Be calm and quiet and kill whatever is causing the stomach pain.

My heart starts pounding, my breathing stops, my hands get sweaty, and I start shaking from the adrenaline. If the noise or threat is directed at me, it can be very dangerous for the person causing the threat.

I am still feeling tense, anxious, and angry.

Lord, ease my pain and fear. Reveal to me what needs to be revealed. Allow me to live in peace within myself.

Tomorrow Mark and I will climb Mt. Charleston; six hours up and four hours down. We are leaving at 5:30 am in the morning.

Praise God and Brother Chuck.

Monday, October 7, 1996

Yesterday Mark, and I and three men from AA, Scott, John, and Larry, climbed to the top of Mt. Charleston. We hiked for a total of nine hours. It was about four and one-half miles up and eleven thousand feet elevation. Mark struggled but made it all the way to the top. We left at 5:30 am and did not get home until 8:30 pm. We enjoyed it even though it was a tough hike. We enjoyed it with the leg cramps and all. I felt proud that Mark hung in there and made it all the way to the top. Next trip we may make it for two days and go over the summit ridge and down the other side.

Tonight I am sitting in Marriott Courtyards in Kansas City for a company staff meeting and computer training. This should be a fun stay. By the way, I made my annual sales objective last week. That means an extra $14,000 or more, for my other compensation. It also means an automatic super achiever club status too.

I should get a check next month for about $50,000! Now that is outstanding!

Tuesday, October 10, 1996

Who would we be
When we would give
What we worship away?
Who would we be
if all our books were
gone?
Who would we be
without our wallets?
Who would we be
without our job,
education, wife, kids,
car, house or that
special little pimple on
our butt?
Can you, for one brief
minute contemplate who
you would be without
any material or mental
possessions?
In this hotel room—nothing
belongs to me. Oh, but
what about the flesh that
you exist in?
This bone
bag we call a body. Isn't

that yours?
"To be or not to be. That
is the question" Isn't it?
Lack of security - that
is our dilemma. If we can
cling to the flesh, then
perhaps it means we won't
die.
Wrong, dumb ass, we will
all die. And we will all
die fairly soon. And we will
all die a lonely miserable
death.
So, screw em and feed em
fish. "It don't mean a
thing"
Just a speck in the distance
as she walks down the
dusty dirt road.
And it don't mean nothing.

Wednesday, October 11, 1996

I am going home tomorrow. It has been one more day on planet earth, as viewed from planet Venus. "I'm just a soldier, a coming home soldier. No purple heart do I wear on my chest."

"The terror of it all for the Vietcong to cut all these little kids arms off just because they had been inoculated by the Americans."

It seems like a long time since my last EMDR session. My

subconscious mind seems to be blocking any thoughts about what has happened or what might happen next time.

I remember the young soldier in Vietnam that quit eating for weeks because he was ingesting so much liquid speed. He was a skeleton. His eyes were sunk deep into their sockets. He had this white crust around his mouth in the days before he died.

Take one night and see it all the way through. This is the only way from point A to point B. I am too tired tonight. I am always too tired to see it through. But I came home didn't I?

"To sleep, perchance to dream. Ah, there is the rub." "Sans sight, sans smell, sans flesh."

Saturday, October 12, 1996

I spent the week in Kansas City. Donna is working overtime again this weekend. She brought home over $1,000 for the past two weeks. Not much new in my job. I made my number and will make a lot of money, but that is about all I know for sure.

I went to the men's AA meeting again this morning and saw Scott and John from our hiking trip. Their egos are something. I feel out of sorts today. I am feeling lonely I guess. Donna and I went to a movie last night. We are going to Bob's 50th birthday tonight. Feel a little apprehensive about that since he drinks but is one of my best customers.

I am not sure why I am writing. I am starting to feel sad right now. Too much. Too much.

Make a lot of money, got a lot of things, can do about anything we want. Still, I feel sad for no reason. Feel rundown, weak, drained. All my fight is gone.

We will be here once and only once. We will never pass this

way again. That seems to be the truth based on our somewhat limited knowledge.

Maybe less coffee and more rest would help.

Monday, October 14, 1996

Today the AA, twenty-four-hour book said, "Don't let the beast in you keep you from your spiritual destiny." Seems appropriate for where I am in this EMDR thing.

I met another veteran named Rick. After seventeen years sober, he had a knee replacement at the VA. They sent him home with massive amounts of drugs. Now after two years of abusing the drugs he ended up in the VA hospital for PTSD. Then after two weeks at the VA, he didn't even know who he was. He went home with another bag of Quaalude's. He overdosed and ended up back in the hospital. This time he nearly died. He is one more Marine that survived Vietnam and has been dying ever since.

I'm still mad at this government for what they did to our troops. I need to be honest about that now. I have been down the road almost fifty years now; it is time to get honest about that.

Another session this afternoon to see if anything is left. Martha also had her gall bladder removed today. Donna just finished working for the third weekend in a row. I need to complete my cabin very soon.

I felt like I was on a roller coaster a few hours ago. The EMDR session covered a lot of ground. This time it seemed like a train ride with many scenes passing by in living color.

So much going on that it is hard to assimilate it on a conscious level, especially this soon after the session. Some of what happened included:

1. Tremendous sadness and feelings of loss.
2. I felt like I abandoned my friends and should have died there with them in Vietnam.
3. Sudden knife strike to my stomach with several ripping gestures. Sadness was stored in my stomach. Suicide attempt was a desire to release my pain.
4. I grieved the loss of a friend who died from speed.
5. I grieved a friend that hung himself.
6. A major fear of going crazy but needed to be crazy to survive and keep people away from me. I recalled the pet scorpion that I had tied on a string.
7. I remember being in Saigon and Bien Hoa. Recalled the firefight at the beer dump.
8. Major reaction to whatever happened in the valley behind the tents during the first few months in country.
9. Recall feeling guilt, shame, fear.
10. Insight into drinking and knife suicide attempt.
11. Tonight I know what survivors guilt is really about.

I feel completely exhausted. My primary emotion seems to be sadness. The session lasted almost two hours. I recall an interruption during the session. I felt angry and had a fear of losing it. With my fingernails, I tore at my face to draw back. I had extreme sensitivity to being touched during the physical reactions. I must maintain an absolute safe area to work.

Memories were very vivid but passed rapidly. I am having physical pain in my neck and stomach. I am concerned about re-opening old wounds and exposing undisclosed events, but I must continue with the process. Tonight I find that I have trust in the process and Dr. Lois. We discussed the trust issue, and I feel better as a result. The pictures are still visible when I close my eyes. This concerns me some.

Tuesday, October 15, 1996

I am having vivid flashbacks. I just got back from taking Mary to school. I saw a little girl walking in the distance. I flashed back to a bunker scene while I was on guard duty. The little Vietnamese girl was walking from God knows where to nowhere. Her head was down, and her feet were bare. She was lost, alone, and homeless.

I remember from yesterday a scene by the river in a restaurant. I remember the firefight behind our tents but cannot visually see the bodies or the blood.

I remember clinging to the chair rather than sitting upright. The middle location is where I want to be. Far left is where the hard work is. The far right location is safe but passive. Integration of self is my goal.

Lots of memories make me feel calm this morning. I am physically relaxed. Memories seem very accessible right now. I am not sure if that is necessarily good.

- Dog's name was Matz. I just remembered that.
- Zeke was the rabid monkey that bit several of my buddies.
- Ground glass in the bottom of our coke bottles was a gift from VC.
- They had little black snails for sale. I used to eat them by the handful.

Memories keep rushing pass. It is so strange. I just need to take a deep breath and go to work now. Write again later.

(Two hours later)

I just remembered that during the session I was making a pattern with my right foot while saying everything must be exactly right. This is the focus and root of the structure. We must make order out of chaos. Even if it is just the movement of a body part, the order must come first then chaos can survive.

Structure, discipline, rigidity, perfectionism, everything has its place. Order is critical when your whole world is blown apart. Tap your fingers in a rhythmic manner. I just saw the face of the man who became a section eight. He was tapping his smoke burnt fingers on the top of the beer can. Day and night, drinking beer while tapping his fingers. That's all he did until they carried him away.

Again I told myself, "I will be strong I will not succumb." I feel the sadness again.

Wednesday, October 16, 1996

It is 5:30 am, and I woke up early. Donna is already off to work. Amazing thing this morning, I woke up without any fear or anxiety. My negative feelings must have left a while ago. I think they left about the time the rashes disappeared. I have had large ring rashes on my thighs and butt for the past several years. They must be stress related because I had them biopsied and no one could explain what they were. What is interesting is that the rashes were mainly located on the side of my thighs and that is where much of my feelings were stuck. Feelings like the fear of not being able to run. So much fear that my legs would not function properly.

For the past couple of weeks the memories have not been accessible but since Monday's session, they, i.e., flashbacks, have been almost continuous. When I close my eyes, I see pictures. I see different people, aircraft sounds, and pictures. Even now while writing I see pictures of Vietnam.

I remembered a .45 caliber pistol we found in the wall of our hooch. We are drinking coke mixed with liquid speed. I am seeing a motorboat spinning around this pool inside my head. I quit using speed that same day.

I remember the 90th replacement battalion. I remember drinking out of a canvas bag for the first time. There is mud everywhere with the fear of the unknown.

Last twenty minutes revisited several scenes in Vietnam. Amazingly, I can see our position at Long Binh before Military Assistance Command Vietnam (MACV) moved there. There was nothing in the valley between us and the hill where MACV would go, except the jungle. We were on a hill. I remember the latrines were the nearest thing to the wire. Old Vietnamese, workers in black pajamas, would drag the half barrels of excrement out and burn them with diesel fuel. There was a creek below us in the forest-covered valley where the VC would attack. Their tunnels were built later during Tet of 1968 on the other side of the perimeter. "Red alert! Red alert! Gook's in the wire!" They would yell. They would always come early in the morning, like at 3:00 am. Ice cold shower from a hanging canvas bag. Now I see the new guys with their pasty white skin, clammy and soft like dead flesh.

I can see it all clearly now. I remember the night they burned Long Binh jail down. We had American prisoners behind us and the Vietcong in front of us. How many soldiers were killed by our own prisoners? I remember they killed some of the guards with wooden tent stakes. Behind us, we had hundreds of out-of-control prisoners inside the perimeter while we were being attacked from the front by NVA troops.

Memories are so dark. They are like the monsoon rain or the darkness of night. There are memories of gloom, despair, heat, sweat, the stench of rotting dead bodies, and diesel fuel. It is hot and humid at night under the mosquito nets. Toss and turn, sleep very light.

Friday, October 18, 1996

I went golfing with customers yesterday. I had a good afternoon. Donna is working until 11:00 pm tonight. She started at six this morning. I feel calm this morning.

Yesterday I was driving down Cheyenne Avenue and saw two men talking by a building. One was wearing a 1st Cav patch on the front of a sleeveless army shirt. As I went by, I noticed the Vietnamese flag on two signs. On one sign was written, "Vietnam Veterans of America." I recalled that I was a member of the first startup group in Minneapolis of the VVA a long time ago.

Saturday, October 19, 1996

Yesterday I was able to identify more feelings. I realized that I was feeling lonely, sad, neglected, and sorry for myself. Donna worked until 10:00 pm last night and had been working four weekends in a row. She is taking all the overtime she can get. Up until a few weeks ago, my fear was the dominant feeling, fear and maybe anger.

I woke up at 3:30 am and realized that I have most likely lost the transmission business. That is valued at over $100 million per year. I think we will hear something next week. My rashes are gone, the fear is less, and Vietnam obsessions have been reduced.

Sunday, October 20, 1996

I just finished doing sitting meditation for the past twenty-five minutes. It felt good to sit on the cushion for a while. Maybe I need to do some cleansing of my body with fruit, vegetables, and water. I have been eating junk food and drinking a lot of coffee lately.

Pure white steamed rice satisfies the soul better than anything else, except perhaps cool spring water from a mountain stream. Maybe I need to visit Chaiya today. Walk quietly, stay away from the TV, and rest this mind and body.

During EMDR, I remembered all the nights I spent alone in the jungle without a rifle. I was wearing black clothes and carrying a knife. The pictures moved by so rapidly that I saw only flashes, but the feelings were also there in bunches and somehow distorted.

I remember crying for all the people I left behind. Grief has been in my stomach while fear is in my chest, shoulders, thighs, and perhaps my wrists.

Yesterday I spoke with Bob T., and he told me that his wife has cancer and they didn't get it all out. She starts chemo this Thursday. He also found out that he has Hodgkin's disease. Wonderful people, I pray for them.

Monday, October 21, 1996

It is 5:30 am, and I had a bad dream. Two dreams actually. The first was about a stainless steel machete. I cannot remember all of the details but I know my boss had bought it and I wanted it. I made him an offer of $454 for it. I just remembered it was not sharp enough, so I took it in to have a really good edge put on it. Woke up briefly.

Next, I dreamed I was trying to kill our yellow cat with a dull knife. I had cut off its tail. Then its back legs at the waist. It was trying to fight back, but I was too strong. I just saw the Viet Cong kids face in Bien Hoa! I could not get the knife through his windpipe. I had to hit it with something. Maybe I was using his machete. I just saw the flesh wound, the blood, and the life go out of his eyes. Getting shock's in my stomach. I must stop writing now.

I am sitting in my office trying to breathe. I have a Buddhist shrine, two sets of beads, two cushions and the brass Buddha I brought home from Vietnam in 1969. I am still able to trance my mind back to the present by controlling my breath. I kept on killing, only now it was animals like deer and birds. I liked the smell of warm blood when I sliced open the deer's stomach cavity and ate several raw organs. I feel sick, weak, tired, and alone. I am alone in the woods.

I stopped breathing now. It's okay. Sitting here in this chair it is okay.

7:30 pm

I'm still here. This is very good news. It has been a tough day. I took my MAC knife and my book on mindfulness and went to the VA for my 8:00 am appointment with the Disabled American

Veterans (DAV) advocate. I sat outside until 7:50 am then went up the front stairs. It was going okay until we started talking about the PTSD claim. Someone slammed a door. I started getting a physical reaction in my stomach and had to leave early. The DAV rep walked me to the stairs. I had a bad time, and I need to go back or meet him somewhere else to get my papers signed to reopen my claim.

I took my MAC knife to the knife man and got it sharpened and buffed. It looks good; it would cut anything now. I left the cell phone off all day. It has been a rough day.

I went to see Dr. Lois. In fact, I called her at 7:00 am and told her about the dream and the face. We talked for almost an hour about the background. I was depressed by the time I got to the session. We did EMDR for about one-half hour, but during that time I relived what happened at the theater. I started by using the machete as the visual image, and my feeling was fear. When I replaced it with the knife, my feelings became rage.

Not sure right now what all happened except I ended up in the left side of the chair with a knife in my right hand. With the blade turned up. I was holding him with my left hand and cut him low in the stomach and ripped the knife upward toward his breastbone.

I experienced terrible fear until that other part of me grabbed hold, and I had a tremendous adrenaline rush as I gutted him. Afterward, I felt really sad; I was asking him why he put me in that position. It was pitch black in the alley outside the theater.

Afterward sitting in a chair, I was sad but also a felt sense of relief that I had faced this thing. A few more EMDR's movements and I think some more stuff will leave my right shoulder.

I am tired tonight. My right hand was so tightly fisted it is still sore. However, I feel like I'm one step closer to being a warm and caring person.

Right now, I feel sad, but I'm sure glad I'm clean and sober and have hope tonight; not the despair I felt most of this day.

Wednesday, October 23, 1996

It is 6:00 am Monday morning. I had a dream that involved people and things in the present but was linked to Vietnam. I dreamt about my boss and a silver machete; the mutilation and killing of our cat, and the killing of the VC at the theater in Bien Hoa.

This morning at 3:24 am, I woke up with the recall of a dream about visiting my friend and AA sponsor Bob T. He found out a couple of months ago that he has Hodgkin's disease. Last week I spoke with him, and he told me that his wife has terminal cancer. She starts chemotherapy tomorrow. I have been sad and angry about that. Bob and I use to drink together in Minneapolis. He has twenty-three years sobriety and is one of my closest friends in the world.

I dreamt that I was at his house where he lived alone. I may have been at his cabin. We were outside talking when he disappeared. I went into the cabin to look for him. He was lying on the bed and told me that he was dying. When I talked to him, he said he had to face his demons, and then his face turned black, and he couldn't breathe. He said that he had killed a man in war and I woke up.

Sunday, January 5, 1997

On New Year's Eve, I spoke with George P., one of only two names I recall from Vietnam. He was the brightest soldier in our unit. He had two years of college. He had the best chance of making it out of Vietnam with his sanity. Now he lives in a small room on State Street in Connecticut. He has never been married, never went back to school, and never held a job. He has been in and out of jail, and he drinks a lot. However, he would never blame it on Vietnam. Many people had it rougher than us over there.

Then he started telling me what a bad time that I had during Tet of 1968. He said I was stuck at the radio relay station until the Viet Cong overran it. I started sweating and had to get off the phone. That was the end of my reunion.

Tuesday, January 7, 1997

Today is a new day. Last night I got angry because a friend of the kids has been around the house too much. Mary told me this morning that she keeps him in the garage because she knows I don't like having him in the house.

The other day he was sitting in my chair in the living room, my looks could have killed. I jumped on Mark a few days ago when he had a house full of friends. I told him that if he didn't get the dishes done, his friends could leave. They all got up and left, Mark with them. Wow! What the hell is wrong with me? Can't my children have friends in the house?

I feel tremendous fear when guys are in the house. I guess I fear a confrontation or something. Or maybe I'm just a self-centered jerk. It doesn't bother me when Mark has Russell over. It is only with the boys that I feel the threat. I wonder if I can change that. One of Marks friends will probably not come back after the scene I created the other day.

Sunday, January 12, 1997

Yesterday was Mark's 18th birthday. I'm sure proud of him. We are very fortunate to have four great kids and four wonderful grandkids. I am feeling very positive today.

This week I have my Compensation & Pension exam (C&P) for PTSD Monday night and Compensation & Pension for prostate cancer Friday afternoon. Also, I am going to Atlanta Tuesday for training. It should be a good week.

Yesterday it occurred to me how well I have been feeling. The depression and sadness have lifted. The Asian obsession is mostly gone too. I am still not clear as to what will be left after all this therapy. I still like my guns though. I have been carrying the loaded 9mm pistol with me when I leave the house.

There will be a lot of change, but I am pretty much focused on today. I feel good today; thank God, I made it through this last year sober and did my therapy without drugs. For an antisocial high school dropout, I am doing okay. This year will also be a very spiritual year for the family and me. Praise God!

I turn fifty this year, and that is a miracle!

Tuesday, January 14, 1997

Tonight I am in Atlanta for product training. Yesterday I had my C&P examination for PTSD. I met with a Chinese shrink for about thirty-five minutes. It was not a good meeting. He was trying to determine what impact, if any, my condition had on my ability to work.

He knew whom I worked for and knew that I made good

money. He was very tactful at setting traps. We were talking about anger, and he asked, "How do you avoid conflict on the job?"

I said, "My boss is in Kansas City, and he only visits occasionally and I work hard to avoid any confrontation."

He said, "So you work hard and are good at your job?"

I snapped back, "I'm good at everything I do!"

This is pretty much the truth. We talked briefly about treatment and my insistence on no drugs and no confinement. He said, "So you never took any anti-depressants." I said, "No, just the anti-anxiety medication and that messed me up, so I put it all in the trash and sought help outside the VA."

He knew I was seeing Dr. Lois and in fact, he had her name, and probably her files on me. My feeling is it did not go well. I was very uncomfortable. My mouth was dry. He questioned why PTSD never came up with Dr. K. in Omaha. I told him he thought it was caused by a screwed up childhood. We spoke briefly about my childhood.

I'm sick of the VA bull-shit. I don't care about their money. I never did. I also told him about the group at the Vet Center in Vegas. I told him the veterans were so screwed up on medications they didn't even know their names.

Friday I go for C&P exams for my cancer. Guess some ex-officer does the exam. He is apparently a jerk and thinks Vietnam Vets are crybabies.

I will go then I am done with it. If I get no money, that's fine. In fact, they can have their $94 per month back too. I risked my life for this country, and so did others, and ever since we have been treated like outcasts, baby killers, and whiners. What I say is, "Screw them all." I will not die! I will not be warehoused! I will not take their drugs! Just leave me alone in peace. Screw them and feed em fish!

****

Its all gone now
there is nothing left.
All form of delusion
smashed like a babies skull.
Empty boxes sitting in
empty rooms.
All symbols, all statues,
all books, all dogma - gone.
Phony people with phony
stories - smashed.
Colors are gone, we
live in a black & white world now.
No flowers, no birds, no
children - only the dead.
And the dead wander
aimlessly.
Death is near - I smell
the stench of rotting flesh.
And that is, as it is.

MARRIAGE SEPARATION

Monday, January 27, 1997

Tonight I sit in San Francisco, the city by the bay. It has been a tough week. Something has been wrong with my relationship with Donna for quite some time. All the intimacy is gone. She has been in a bad place ever since starting the job.

I don't know what all happened on the job. I guess it was rough on her. We had a bad falling out in Denver, and since then it just isn't getting any better. This past week my job was hectic too. We had thirty people in from the main office for a quality control meeting. Therefore, I had dinner, shows, and golf all week.

Saturday night we went to dinner at Hugo's with my boss and his wife. We also had a customer and her husband with us too. That seemed to go all right, but Donna was in a hurry to get the evening over.

Afterward, I asked her if she wanted to stop somewhere.

She said, "No I just want to go home; I'm tired." After we got home, she asked me, "Would you mind if I go out with the girls?"

I said, "I thought you were tired and if not why didn't you want to go out with me earlier."

Anyway, I got upset and left and got home about 2:00 am. She didn't go anywhere. I sat in my office until 6:00 am trying to figure this situation out.

Friday night I touched her in bed, and I get this cold brush off. Anyway, last night I told her we needed to talk about what is going on. She said she needs time and space to figure out what she wanted to do. She had told me before that I hurt her when I asked Clare if she thought Donna had ever been unfaithful to me.

Last night I told her that she needed to decide whether she wanted to be here or not. She said, "I am here." Anyway, last night, later, in bed we talked about the situation. She admitted that she has been spending time in malls and parks trying to figure out what she wanted to do about our relationship.

She said that I have never been there to support her emotionally. And, I don't trust her and probably don't trust anyone. She also admitted that her situation has changed because she now has a job where she can support herself.

We talked about my fears about her. She said she does not want to hurt anyone and has been worried about my reaction. I told her the worst case scenario we would have was to split everything up and go our own way. But, I told her that I didn't want that to happen. I said I was willing to do whatever she thought was necessary to stay together.

She mentioned having thought about seeing someone. I encouraged her to do that if she wanted to. It feels like it is over. She said she had been emotionally numb for quite a while. She also said she is not looking for another guy and has not thought about the details of moving out.

We also talked about my recurring impotence after my prostate cancer surgery. She said sex did not have anything to do with it. That it was simply that I have never been there for her emotionally. It was also the trust issue. I told her that I could understand why she would want to leave. She is financially independent, and I cannot support her emotionally or sexually.

She said it was not just the recent incident in Omaha, but that I had never been there for her and never trusted her. My lack of trust mainly is when she is working. I told her about my fears and insecurities. This morning she came into my office, kissed me goodbye, patted me on the shoulder, and said have a good trip.

I am hurt, angry, and fearful right now. I have no one to blame but myself. I feel that I do have some strengths and assets. This is not a perfect world, and I have not been a perfect husband or father. The truth is that she is right. I have never been there for her emotionally. I spend ninety percent of my home time in my room alone. I eat in my room, and I sleep in my room. I have been isolated for a very long time. Now I will reap the consequences.

I called my sponsor from the airport and also spoke with Dr. Nancy. I am alone in my room now, and there is a big party going on downstairs for the achievers club. Yes, I am a super achiever and in the "Achievers Club," but I am still a dumb ass.

The relationship feels dead tonight. When I touch her, she pulls away. When I speak to her, she is condescending. Are twenty-six years of marriage about to end? I am also worried about her. I have never seen her this way. She is totally shut down. I keep thinking it cannot all be me. I have been a jerk most of my life. I am searching for what else it could be.

She has indicated that she is bored. The other night she mentioned that we had been married since she was eighteen. I think she needs to have some fun. She wants to try to make it on her own. Enjoy life a little. She said several times that life is too short. "I am not going to do this anymore." Maybe she is right.

I mean look at me. I don't drink or smoke, and I am not able to have sexual intercourse. What the hell is left? I feel really defeated tonight.

Tuesday, January 28, 1997

Well, it is another day in the life of a salesman. I went to a golf clinic today. I had a good day considering I didn't speak to the woman I have lived with the last twenty-six years.

I met an interesting guy by the name of Ed at the golf course today. He is the top lawyer in my company. We had a nice talk on the bus on the way to the golf course. Then we ended up sitting across from each other tonight on the ride back from the company outing. It turns out he was in Vietnam in 1969 working in SOG intelligence near Nha Trang. He and I had a lot in common. He was a nice person. I hope to see him again tomorrow.

I did not call Donna last night or tonight. I guess I need some time to think all this stuff out too. I am angry, hurt, and being stubborn. I had trouble sleeping last night because of thinking about all this stuff. I cannot believe it. I guess I don't believe she would ever leave me. I can only hope I'm right. It is getting late. I will write again tomorrow.

Wednesday, January 29, 1997

It is two days before the beginning of Tet 1968, and I am hurting in a really bad way. It feels like I have lost everything. If I die tonight, I want my kids to know how much I love them.

Donna, you have been the best thing that ever happened in my life. I will always love you. I am sorry I was unable to be the person you needed me to be. You have stayed with me longer than anyone should have and I thank you for that. I realize now how sick I have been. It has been especially harmful to my family. I am sorry for that. Even now, the words of love do not come to me. I died a long time ago.

Later. I went downstairs, talked to my boss and feel much better. One thing I am finding out is how much inner strength I have. I ended up going to an AA meeting. It is the one thing that has always worked for me. If I drink, I am dead. They are the same thing.

I just got back from sitting with a friend the past couple of hours. I think everything will be all right.

Tuesday, February 4, 1997

I am in Orlando doing some more writing. I am tired tonight. I got up early this morning and have been busy politicking all week. Donna and I are getting along better.

I saw Brother Chuck last night, but I am too tired to go over there tonight. He preached pretty strong to me yesterday anyway. I dislike the guilt that organized religion tries to lay on us. I do not have much else to write about tonight. I started working for Andrew again this week. It is strange to be working for him again. Oh well, I still don't have a promotion either.

I started taking medications from the VA this week on Feb 1st. I'm taking it twice a day per the doctor's orders. So far, I have not had any side effects. They are supposed to be non-addictive. I told Donna I was going to try this crap for a few weeks to see if it makes any difference in my behavior, but I don't feel any different.

I guess it takes a few weeks before they start to work. Oh well, stuff happens.

Wednesday, February 5, 1997

I am ready to go home. I am feeling sad this morning. I am so sick of all this change. I have another new job with a completely different team. I felt out of place with the wireless team last night. I ended up sitting by myself at dinner. I am going to miss the people from the last sales team. I will especially miss James and Pat. It seems like there is no stability in my life anymore. Everything is always changing. I am so tired of it all.

I have a two o'clock flight this afternoon, but I don't get home until 7:30 pm tonight. Then Friday it is off to a weekend of golf with the company team. I am supposed to take a customer, George with me down to Lake Havasu.

I was supposed to go golfing this morning but I didn't bring my shoes or clubs. So I sit on my butt until I catch a plane. I only play golf because it is a required part of this sale job. It is just more stress for me. It sucks. I am sick of people trying to change me too.

My close friends on the sales team are gone. The rest have been split up and placed on different teams. I feel out of place with this new team. I feel out of place with the new customer. I feel out of place in my own damn house. (However, I am working on that.)

I took my medication a little while ago and started to feel tingling in my hands and a little dizzy. I am chewing Copenhagen snuff again maybe that is what is making me feel dizzy. I need to make some decisions about my trips. Life sucks. I feel emotionally shut down. I need to rest.

Tuesday, February 11, 1997

I thought I would write from home for a change. The last couple of days I have been struggling with bouts of anger and sadness. During the day, the medication seems to help, but I have been waking up at 3:25 am in the morning with the sweats again. I cannot remember the dreams, but I know this is the time of the year that everything went to hell over in Vietnam. This is about the time that we were trying to hold the radio relay station from enemy attacks.

There isn't much else going on. Donna is going to Kansas City to see Sara this Friday. Sunday I am going to Ohio for more training. I will be gone all next week. There is not much of a life with all this travel.

My good friend Brother Chuck messed up big time. He called Donna this last Friday night looking for me. I guess they had quite a talk. He told her about the medication and how much I was isolating. And he said what I needed to do was "Standup and be a man!"

As far as I am concerned, Brother Chuck no longer exists. I sent him an e-mail telling him he had violated my confidence and that he could keep his stupid advice. End of topic. By Monday, I will have forgotten his face.

Sonny called last night too trying to probe as to what is going on. I said very little. I don't trust him anymore either. Screw them all! There is nobody left that I can trust.

Sunday, February 16, 1997

I am sitting in Dublin, Ohio waiting for the sun to come up. There isn't much going on this early in the morning. It was a long flight from Las Vegas. I spent a half hour working out on the stair climber and took my morning pills.

Donna is in Kansas City seeing our new granddaughter. She seems to be doing better, but she is still acting strangely. I spoke with Jimmy A. for a while today. He is a good man. He has had many problems too. He just busted his leg by falling out of his wheelchair. God knows I could have it a lot worse. My friend Rick, the Marine, found out his wife of seventeen years has brain and lung cancer. He is really shook up over it. He didn't say anything about it in the AA meeting yesterday though. We did talk for a while at breakfast.

I was thinking about a gratitude list on the plane ride over. It might not be a bad idea:

1. I am still married to a wonderful woman.
2. I have four healthy and wonderful, children.
3. I have a great job.
4. I paid off $9k credit card last month.
5. The car and house is our only debt.
6. I am cancer free.
7. I am sober, by the grace of God.
8. I have four healthy, wonderful, grandkids.
9. We have $130k in 401K.
10. We have $40k in equity.
11. We have forty acres of land in Minnesota.
12. I have people that care about me.
13. I have a wonderful AA fellowship.
14. I have a guaranteed retirement.

It is amazing what a little gratitude list will do for you. Huh? Not much else to write about tonight. I will be here until Friday. Next week I am in New Jersey and Kansas City. The following week

I will be in Orlando. I am busy all the time, but that is the way it is supposed to be.

Tuesday, February 25, 1997

It is another crappy day on the road. I went to an AA meeting with my new boss today. We had a good meeting and a chat afterward. It was weird because everyone on our team wondered where we disappeared to after dinner. We are in Morristown N.J. It is a nice place to visit, but I wouldn't want to live here.

I just got off the phone with my other half. She didn't have much to say. She has a headache. She must be tired of dealing with all the stuff at home and work again.

I placed a thousand dollars down on a log cabin in Minnesota. I should hear from them sometime this week. There isn't much going on besides that today. I have been fussing a bit over whether or not to finance that much for the cabin. Oh well, we only live once, and I need a place to call home that is paid for.

I am still taking the pills and seeing Dr. Nancy at the VA. I am not sure what that is about, but the antidepressants do seem to be helping some. Tomorrow I will be going to Kansas City. I am looking forward to seeing the kids and some of my friends in the program.

I am feeling sad over my poor relationship with Donna. It still is not right and what is worse is that I do not know what is wrong. The pills do seem to help me focus on the present rather than speculate. That's it for now.

Sunday, March 2, 1997

I have been on medication for thirty days, and it is a good thing because it has been crazy around the house and the job. I feel like writing some poetry tonight here in Orlando.

My Mother
Eight barefoot kids huddled
around a potbelly stove.
Eight barefoot kids sleeping
in one bed.
Eight barefoot kids on wood
floor. (one on his hands and knees)
Dog named Spotty running
free "To the woods!"
Cold, hungry, nights in the
north woods of Minnesota.
Mom, why do you come
home drunk so much?
You know everyone
in Deer Creek is talking
about you sitting up there
at Henderson Corner bar.
Mom, don't hang on us
when you smell of whiskey
and smoke.
Mom, I'm sorry it was such
a struggle. I love you, Mom.
My Wife
Donna, when you were only
eighteen we got married. It has

not been easy for you. I am
sorry you have had to carry
the work load so long.
You are the reason I
stay alive.
You mean so
much to me. I will
always love you. No
matter what. There can
be no other. Nothing
else matters to me.
You are changing now.
You need space and time
to figure it out.
You told me, "You have
never been here for me
emotionally. You never trusted
me, and you have always
been alone"
These words hurt me
deeply. If they are true,
then I cannot go on.
My purpose for living is over.
but, I have faith that every
thing will be all right. We
will make it through this time,
and we will be together always.
I will change. You have
opened my eyes. My only
fear is that your love for
me is already dead.

Even if this is true, please
stay. We must grow old
together. It is as it should
be.
And, even so, if you
must go to follow your
singular path. I will
wait. As you have
waited for me these
twenty-six years.
Bless you for being
with me all this
time. You truly
are a God send.
I love you, Honey.

Wednesday, March 12, 1997

It feels like the world is falling apart. Donna is moving out and taking Mary with her. I am not doing well right now. I am hurt and angry. She keeps telling me that I am the problem. She says the kids cannot even have friends over to the house without me wanting to take their heads off.

I'm staying on the Nevada state line headed south to California. I will see our Vietnamese family friends and Mr. Lee and figure out what to do from there. I am very sad. I have nowhere to go. I have no one left to trust or care for. Headed south, I am completely alone in this hotel.

I spoke with Donna this morning, and she is determined to

separate. I might be the one leaving. I cannot bring myself to think about it much. My boss knows about it, and that is it.

I saw a lawyer yesterday. His wife had left him three weeks ago. He was sitting at his desk hung over with his head in his hands. He was so devastated that he couldn't even begin to give me advice. I got up and walked out of his office. I guess I need to find a different lawyer.

I need a few days away from everything and may check myself into the VA psychiatric ward. I do not know how to deal with what is happening to me. I have to leave now. I will not drink or kill myself over this thing.

Thursday, March 13, 1997

I am alone at another rundown hotel. I called Donna this morning and suggested that I come home and try to work it out. She said that I would be trying to push and control the situation. I suggested separate bedrooms and maybe seeing a counselor. She said she has been talking to her Mom, Betsy, and her brothers. She needs time away from me to decide what she wants to do. She said she needs at least a month.

I told her that if I stayed gone that long one of us would not want to get back together and it would be over. She said she has a lot of old resentments and new ones like the lawyer and VA medications. She said if she went with me to see a counselor, it would be just to appease me.

I just tried to get a ticket out of the country. I have been acting Vietnamese for the last several days. I must be going through some kind of regression because I am speaking Vietnamese, thinking

Vietnamese and dreaming in Vietnamese. It takes ten days to get a visa to Vietnam or I would probably be gone already.

I spoke with Mr. Lee and his son at length. They told me to see Linh Bac Si Dau (Army head doctor), so I called Dr. Nancy at the VA. She told me to go to VA psychiatric ward for a week and to quit calling Donna. She said I should just leave her alone as she has asked. So tonight I sit not far from my family and my house, but totally alone.

Rick, from my AA group, will take me to Nellis VA Hospital in the morning and take my car for the week. I don't know what I will do or where I will go after my stay in the hospital. I guess I will either get an apartment or leave the country suc doi (forever).

Tonight I am despondent. Don't have any family. Don't have a house. Very sad. Want to go back to the Republic of Vietnam.

VA PSYCHIATRIC WARD CONFINEMENT #1

Friday, March 14, 1997

Psychiatric ward day one: Rick gave me a ride over at 8:30 am this morning. It has been a difficult day. I feel very anxious in this place. I met with the doctor when I checked in, and he was asking me stupid questions like what was going on that brought me here. Then he asked one of the dumbest questions ever. He asked what I did in Vietnam while I was there. I could not even come up with an answer to that question. After the doctor was through asking questions, I met with a team of people, and they asked me a series of the same questions. After that was finished, they had me take a bunch of written tests. I could only eat one meal today because of the stress.

I am feeling a little more comfortable tonight. Earlier I started crying while I was lying on my bed thinking about my family. The day nurse, Julie, was helpful and is easy to talk to. She did one of the interviews when I first got here. Also, the night nurse, Jan, let me take a walk outside with her. I was able to speak with her about some things. She said that she was separated after thirty-three years of marriage. I am feeling a little more at ease tonight.

I do not know where I am going to go when I get out of here. I heard voices earlier in the nurse's station that sounded Vietnamese. That might be because I have felt I was back in Vietnam all week. I am thinking that way right now. I am feeling very tense and sad about my life.

Saturday, March 15, 1997

Psychiatric ward day two: Not speaking to my family is the most difficult thing I have ever had to do. I have not talked to Donna or the kids on the phone since last Thursday morning. I left the house last Tuesday morning.

One of the reasons it is so hard is because I have to look at how dependent I have become on my relationship with Donna. I have not been more than a call away from her in almost twenty-six years. I guess that can be construed as control by either or both of us. For sure, my rigidity and negativity affected my relationship with Donna and the kids and probably everyone else as well. Once again, I am focused on myself.

It is a long day today, and I want to call and let them know I am all right. However, according to Dr. Nancy, that may be trying to influence or manipulate her behavior, so, for the time being, I will leave her alone.

I slept very little last night. I woke up in a sweat after about an hour's sleep and continued to jump at every noise or movement the rest of the night. This morning was rough. I had a crying spell, and a lot of stress, about uniformed military people entering our sector. When I saw them coming down the hall, I squatted down against the wall and began speaking in Vietnamese. The people here are helpful and understanding.

Sunday, March 16, 1997

It is getting to be another long day. My feelings keep going from rage to sadness back to rage. I cannot imagine what it would be like without the antidepressants. I have been thinking about Donna a lot today. I want to list the signs that led up to this situation and try to figure out what is really going on with her.

I am feeling really bad about not calling them. I hope everything is all right. I will call Martha tomorrow morning and check to see if everything is all right. It has been tough on me, and I am sure tough on them as well.

I keep wondering if I will be able to live alone if necessary. I keep trying to stay in the present, but it is difficult. I only slept five hours total the last two nights. The staff suggested taking a sleeping pill but so far, I have declined. My startle reflex has been wild. I actually feel sounds in my body before they hit my ears and the sounds are making me jump like crazy.

I still don't feel like there is much hope for me. My experience seems so different from most veterans. I still feel more Vietnamese than American most of the time. I feel lost and tired.

Last night I woke up with sweat on my back again; even the sheet was damp. I had a dream that I was USMC Private First Class Bobby Garwood, the last American POW who was later court-martialed and found guilty of collaborating with the enemy. I was eating, sitting, sleeping, talking, and walking in Vietnamese. I was in a jungle camp squatted down eating rice with fish sauce. It was nighttime hot, humid, with bugs everywhere. Suddenly in the dream, I realized that I had forgotten how to speak English. I awoke with a physical snap reflex and sat straight up in bed.

I keep wondering when it all started and when it will end. The staff spoke to me about Mineral Park, California PTSD treatment program today. I do not know if I am ready for confinement in some treatment center. I am just worried about making it through this week. I had a major outburst in anger management class today. I hate it when people try to tell you about anger instead of just letting you display the crap and get it off your chest. The stupid class was on how to communicate anger safely. I know how to communicate anger. I told them that Bruce Lee said, "If you touch me, I will bruise your flesh, if you bruise my flesh, I will break your bones, if you break my bones, I will kill you."

I told them some of us were trained that if someone gets in your face, you take them out with no display of anger. I had a physical rush go through my body when I spoke. It felt like a rush of rage. I hope I am better able to handle the group tomorrow.

Monday, March 17, 1997

I am feeling better tonight because I had a call from Martha earlier. She called my boss and found me. I just checked my cell phone messages, and the mailbox was full of messages from Donna and the kids. Donna was getting progressively angrier each time she left a message. I don't know where this will end, but I know that I am really dependent on her. I can understand why she has felt smothered all these years. Meanwhile, I had another panic attack this morning. I couldn't even breathe and kept crying and slipping away. The nurses said that I was disassociating. I slept a little better last night. I got about four hours of sleep.

I hope I can get some help while I am here. I met with another psychiatrist last Friday and clashed with him. Today I met with the staff team. It has been a busy day, and I am feeling exhausted right now.

Tuesday, March 18, 1997

I had another panic attack with disassociation again today. It happened during the first few minutes of the PTSD group. I started hyperventilating along with physical jerking of my legs. My body became so stiff I was unable to walk. Someone helped me get out of the room. It was a very rough time. I stayed spaced out for a couple of hours afterward.

I called Donna for the first time a little while ago. We talked about what is going on. She said she is still really angry. I told her I would take her lead on whether or not I come home. She said it seemed apparent that I could not handle being gone. She is looking at her own stuff as to why she has stayed in the relationship as long as she has. She said she must have been getting something out of it.

Anyway, I probably need to stay gone for a month for her sake. I tried to call back to the house, but there was no answer. I am exhausted again tonight. I found out today that I will be attending a combat PTSD group at the clinic when I get out.

Wednesday, March 19, 1997

I had another panic attack yesterday during PTSD group session. I had a complete loss of body control, hyperventilated, crying and disassociation. When I disassociated, it felt like I would never be able to make it back. It felt like a safe place to be zoned out in psychosis. I can understand the benefits of being insane. I was spacey for a couple of hours afterward. At least I didn't end up in the bunker back in Vietnam.

This morning I had sweaty palms and anxiety, but I was able to talk to a staff person before it escalated out of control. This morning I managed to make it through PTSD group, but again I expressed a lot of anger at the facilitator.

I received some results from the test they did when I first got here. The tests included the Minnesota Multiphasic Personality Inventory (MMPI), the Shipley-2 and others that I cannot remember. The test results were very revealing. The psychologist listed my symptoms. Line after line it uncovered chronic PTSD with disassociation and physical reactions. They also had some new terms like isolation, minimal effect, so on and so on.

Even with all that bad news, I feel pretty good this evening. I am getting out on Friday. I'm apprehensive about the marriage situation, but I will be glad to be home with the kids. Tonight, I am glad that Dr. Nancy was able to get me in here. I feel like I am starting a new journey. I do not know where it is going but believe, with God's help, I will be all right.

Thursday, March 20, 1997

Well, I thought I was going home tomorrow, but I got a call from Dr. Nancy this morning, and she urged me to stay until the middle of next week. This is my second day without a flashback or panic attack. I feel normal today. I am sad because Donna is moving into her apartment tonight.

It is a strange world in which we live. We never know where

we are going. It was suggested in the group today that we write a gratitude list tonight. So:

- I am sober and clean
- I will always have my kids
- I have a good job
- Money in the bank
- A house, car
- No prostate cancer
- Some awareness about PTSD
- People that care about me
- Food, and my land
- Good memories of our marriage
- The hope for a continued relationship

I am tired tonight. I hope I can get a good night sleep. I will pray for Donna tonight. I hope you can forgive me for the harm I have caused you, and maybe someday you will remember our good times together. I miss you tonight.

Saturday, March 22, 1997

It has been a very long day today. George scared the hell out of me a couple of hours ago. He was standing near my bed looking at me when I woke up. I had a major startle reflex. I felt like I was about to be attacked. I am still in a disassociated fog because of the incident.

I saw Mark last night. He came to visit me at the hospital. The visit went well. I was supposed to see the other kids today, but I suggested we wait until I get out Monday. I spoke with Donna last night too. I told her that I would like to see her today, but after more discussion, we decided that might not be such a good idea right now.

I am still feeling isolated and alone. I do not know if that will ever go away. I may never trust another human being after this mess.

I slept all night but woke up briefly about 4:30 am. This afternoon I took an hour nap. Only one more night in this place and then I am out of here. I will need to spend some time looking at what happens when I leave. I am pretty apprehensive about being alone in the house next week. I am terrified of it. That is why I talked to Mark last night. He will be there with me. Martha is going to Kansas City Monday night for a week.

Intellectually I know what is happening is for the best because we could not go on as we were. However, the last few months have been very rough.

Sunday, March 23, 1997

It is another beautiful morning from the VA psych ward. I finally had a good night's sleep. I slept from 11:00 pm to 5:00 am this morning. I needed the rest. One more night here and it is back to the real world. Today should go faster because we have some groups to attend.

Last night I tried to call Donna at seven o'clock, but there was no answer. I begin to worry or obsess about where she is whenever I try to call her, and she is not there. I do not know if that is obsessive behavior, worry, a need to control, or dependency. I think it is probably a need to control. Whatever it is, it is sure hard to let it go. I need to find a way to get over this control issue because it is driving her out of my life. The theory is that I must be okay without her before she is okay with me.

I think that if I do not have her phone number or address, it will be easier to stay away from her. I will let her call me when she is available to talk, or maybe I need to refocus my energy on new things to do like:

- Stay busy at night.
- Stay gone.
- Learn to deal with her not answering the phone.
- Let go.
- Accept that she needs a life.
- Not question where she has been.
- Arrange a time to see her or call her. Control?
- I was also thinking about work. Should I go back immediately, or wait a few days? I need to reconnect with someone. I have no one left that I can trust, or maybe I never had anyone.
- I feel homesick for tonight.
- I feel no roots or continuity in my life.
- I feel socially isolated and alone.
- I lack faith in God right now.
- I feel a lack of direction.
- I am self-obsessed.
- I feel unworthy of living.

I need to get out of myself. Maybe I can work with others while working on my PTSD crap. Still, there is a beautiful sunrise this morning. It will be a good day. This will be my last day in the VA psych ward.

I have been thinking about home security, my inability to sleep, and aloneness when I get home. I feel like crying, even now. All my words about being born alone, living alone, and dying alone seem painfully accurate today. I am so glad that my son Mark will be there when I get home. I hope he does not leave. I need him right now.

INFIDELITY AND ANGER

Thursday, March 27, 1997

I have been home from the psych ward since Monday. It has not been easy. Donna has moved to an apartment. I have not seen her since March 10th. We have only spoken on the phone a couple of times.

I saw Dr. Lois yesterday. I am having trouble concentrating on anything right now. I will have dinner with Donna tomorrow night at 7:00 pm. I sure hope we can work it out because this is making me crazy. I am sad despite taking 300mg of antidepressants a day. I have to think of the kids now. I have been praying foxhole prayers morning and night.

Monday I received notification the VA increased my disability to sixty percent based on my agent-orange exposure. That is a total of $777 per month because the military decided to poison me while I was in Vietnam. It can be up to $900 depending on the number of dependents.

I have appealed the "No increase on PTSD" part. I even get $74 for the loss of a creative body organ. The loss of my manhood is worth $74?

I guess I'm feeling a little angry today. Oh well, I miss my wife a lot.

Saturday, March 29, 1997

I have been reviewing the relationship changes in my journal for the past hour. I am home alone tonight. Mary has moved into the apartment with Donna.

Donna and I had dinner last night, and it was a very strained conversation. She does not want to put a time limit on the separation, and she is not willing to get counseling either. She said she is not seeing anyone but would not rule it out. She looked tired and puffy eyed. She said she is not sleeping well because of the noise and being in a different bed.

Man, I do not know what is going on. I'm confused, hurt, and angry and so is she. But right now she is not willing to try to save our twenty-six-year marriage.

Jenny just called, and we talked for quite a while. I just took my medications.

Sunday, March 30, 1997

Easter Sunday. I called Donna and talked for a while this morning. She told me the following:

1. She still cares about me.
2. She will date if asked but is not looking for a relationship.
3. She felt like she has been my mother.

4. She thinks I should date.
5. She thinks life is too short.
6. She is not thinking of divorce.
7. I should have some fun. I'm too serious.
8. She wanted to know if I would like to go to a movie with her and the kids.

I feel sick to my stomach right now. I don't want a date! I want my wife back! I'm confused, angry, hurt and I don't know what else. Yesterday I was raging, and earlier today I felt okay. Now after talking to Donna, I am hurt and upset again.

Maybe I do need to stay away from her for a while. However, if I stay away, I may lose her. And if I'm there, I don't have her. And if I am there, I am trying to manipulate the situation.

Wednesday, April 9, 1997

I had dinner with Donna, my sister Jenny, and her husband Dean last night. I can feel it all slipping away. After dinner, Donna and I sat and talked for a while; her body language at dinner was leaning away from me. She said that maybe we ought to sell the house, split the money, and each buy a little house. That way if we get back together we could sell one or rent it out. It sure didn't make a lot of sense to me.

She is also still talking about getting a different apartment with a six-month lease. I told her I guess it depends on her short-term goals because if she plans to get back together her current living situation is fine. If she were looking to be on her own long-term, then an unfurnished apartment would be cheaper and more comfortable.

Every time I meet with her, I get more confused. I just cannot figure it out. I don't know what to do. I feel powerless and out of control. I am still having trouble sleeping and took a sleeping pill last night. That is the first sleeping pill I have taken since I got out of the hospital. At least I slept until 6:30 am this morning.

I don't even know what I want out of all of this relationship stuff. It is too messy. Maybe I will write some of my options:

1. Wait and see up to six months.
2. Want her to come home and want to be here.
3. Reach settlement and divorce.
4. Divorce and let the chips fall.
5. Retire and screw it all!
6. Live on the street.
7. Get drunk!
8. Kill myself!
9. Leave it all alone.
10. Move by myself to Kansas City or Ohio.

Monday, April 14, 1997

It is another day in the life of this wandering soul. I am in Orlando for a company staff meeting. There isn't much going on, except I am no longer living with my wife of twenty-six years.

I can't figure it out. I don't know when it all started to go bad. I have been on a damn roller coaster for the past month. I keep going between sadness, hurt and rage. The last few days it has been pretty much just rage.

I received my sixty percent disability for agent-orange induced cancer a week ago. Big deal! I don't feel like working, eating, or being around anyone. I especially don't feel like being around the kids, and they are the ones that are hurt the most in this situation. I keep looking at options. I only have two. The first is to wait out the six months and hope she decides to come back. The second is divorce her and get on with my life. I would have done the second already if I had any reason to believe she is not entirely faithful to me. I do not want to dwell on that possibility too much. In fact, I won't even allow myself to look at that possibility right now.

It is hard, emotionally, to see her or talk to her on the phone. I saw her last Tuesday night with Dean and Jenny. It was a very strained visit and didn't go well at all. She was wondering if we ought to sell the house and split the money. That hurts. Everything we have worked for our entire life is at risk. The stability of the family is already destroyed. I don't know how much more I can take emotionally.

I saw Dr. Nancy last Wednesday. She gave me some good advice. She suggested that I get rid of the AK-47's, quit Muy Thai kickboxing, and leave Donna alone. She said it would not be good for me to go into a PTSD treatment program at this time. She said my psychological condition would not do well in a confined VA environment. I think she is right.

I have asked Martha to move out of the house so she can be closer to her school. She and Mark are getting an apartment on the first of May. Soon I will be completely alone. As Donna said, I can live in my crystalline world alone.

I could move to Minnesota and live in an underground bunker on my land. I'm about done working anyway. I cannot go on much longer; the pain is too much. I can't see the road ahead. I feel lost and all by myself.

I still may leave the country. I have some unfinished business in Vietnam that needs to be wrapped up. Now would be a good time to do that, and the sooner, the better, I guess. Nobody needs to know, and nobody cares anyway.

I feel weary and vulnerable tonight. I cannot walk this road sober much longer. All the delusion is gone. There is nothing left to live for. It has all been destroyed. The family is gone, and all material objects are gone. Only the job is left, and that will go soon enough.

I need a way to sleep. Maybe I need eternal sleep, beneath that lonely willow tree just west of Deer Creek Minnesota in the grave-yard just north of the road.

- long time,
- sad time,
- empty time,
- weary time.
- All is lost. All is gone.
- All is gone except silence and everlasting sleep in the ground with the worms eating my rotting flesh, and maggots crawling in my empty eye sockets. Even now, I can smell the stench.

THE PSYCHOTIC BREAK

Wednesday, April 15, 1997

Today is the hungry ghost day. What I must do becomes more evident as time slips away. I must leave this culture and never return. I do not belong here; I never did and I never will. It was all a mistake, a bad mistake that lasted almost fifty years.

There is another place. It was before this place, and it will be after this place. That is where I belong. I will not be alone there. My mother and father will be there. It will be quiet, and everything will move slowly. The people will walk with grace and not know material wealth. My head will be held high. Time will move slowly and will be unending. There will be sadness there, but no one will be left alone to feel it.

When I was a young man in this world, there was much pain and aloneness. Sitting alone as a child near the top of the oak tree, I knew there was another place. Walking alone beside my dog Spotty, I knew it could be different. However, today, I have the choice to go there. There is nothing left for me here. It has all been destroyed. Perhaps a shaved head and robe awaits me. I do not know. It is hard to know. I am sad, alone, empty, forgotten, and abandoned by the only person that was always there.

People are material objects. They are nothing else, Just flesh and blood, nothing else, bones that will decay with time. Nevertheless, this day is my day. I must act and do what is undone. Time is running out. It must be done now, this very week. Perhaps this very day.

Saturday, April 26, 1997

Happy Birthday to me! It is 1:00 am in the morning, and I am sitting in my home bunker with my sleeping bag, Buddha statues, AK-47's, 9mm pistol, and a ton of ammo. Oh, I forgot the meditation cushion, knives, and miscellaneous military equipment. The door is secured with a new deadbolt keyed lock. There is a black sheet over the small window. The exterior perimeter is safeguarded with locks and darkness. Silence has become my friend once again.

I moved out of the master bedroom into this small room for security reasons. Everyone is gone. I am alone now with only my weapons. The chain is broken. The three knots untied. But even as I write, other chains are being mended. Dr. Nancy calls it posttraumatic stress regression. I call it survival.

Yesterday was a rough day for me. It was April 24th, our 26 wedding anniversary. I sat alone in a five bedroom, three-bath house near the lake in sin city planet earth.

I last saw "*she*" on April 8th. *She* called last Thursday and wanted to know if we were going to have a cake and get together for Mary's birthday. My response was, "No, I have my own cake and ice-cream for her." Many things are happening that I cannot write about. Suffice to say there will be life after *she*.

Perhaps it ended the day *she* said *she* was considering leaving me. Perhaps it was later. However, it is broken now.

Twenty-six years ago, we placed rings on each other's fingers. They were supposed to symbolize commitment, trust, and, perhaps, love. Twenty-six years later the ring is broken, the trust is broken, the commitment is broken, and the ring is off.

But I will not break. I will survive once again. I survived childhood, Vietnam, cancer, death, and now this. I will survive!

Thirty years of playing the game. I never wanted to be in this culture. I never liked it here. I never fit. I never bought into the bullshit. I only adapted temporarily to survive. Play the game. Wear the suit. Screw-them all, screw them ALL!

Cause it don't mean nothing.

- Discipline is all that matters now.
- Structure.
- Conformity.
- Calculating rational thought.
- No Emotions.
- Be alone.
- Be alone and keep calm.
- Breathe in, breathe out.
- Look within for that dark side that knows how to deal with anything.

And above all sleep on the floor for the simple life. He came with nothing and no one. He will leave same, same.

Sunday, April 27, 1997

Today is this day. It is none other than this day. I just finished scaring the hell out of my friends at the 80th street AA club. They must think I have gone off the deep end for sure, but all I did was tell them the truth about where I am right now. And where I am is a little scary.

It feels different here in Kansas City. The green grass seems reassuring to my soul. The trees give me strength. Even the clouds feel cooler than the sun. In Vegas, it is the sun every day. It is the sun every day. It is none other but the sun every day.

In a very uneventful way yesterday, I turned fifty. I had a small cake and a few gifts from the kids. Mark and I went to kickboxing last night. That was quite enjoyable. One of my friends from our Muy Thai class was fighting. I don't recall what I wrote the last time. I guess it was something about "happy, joyous and free" or some happy stuff like that. I have hives really bad on the back of my right leg and inside my right elbow. I am not sure what that means, but it is not good.

I have some Vietnam pictures with me. They are old Vietnam pictures; old and dead pictures. I am going back to visit the graves, to see the ghosts, walk the paths, and kill the dead people. I must stop the dead ones from following me around.

I try to talk to Buddha about it, but he does not understand. He tells me I must be more disciplined. I must:

- Walk quieter.
- Talk less.
- Eat less.
- Sleep less.
- Sex less.
- Touch less.
- Be less.
- Live less.
- Die more.

Now, where was I? Does it matter, or does it not matter? Or does it matter, or does it not matter? Is it less? Or is it, perhaps, more? Then when it was time to cut cut, there was more blood blood.

My question for today is, "Are we powerless?" In AA, we say we are powerless. God has all power. God's greatest power is to give life and take life. I can give life. I can take life. I can take my own life. I can take your life. Ergo I am God.

Monday, April 28, 1997

Yes, it is another day in the life of Michael. One thing I am finding out about myself is that I cannot keep my mouth shut about anything. I spent the evening with some people from 80th street and started blabbing about my plans. I was just speaking stupid stuff. Most of what I said didn't even make sense. I was just talking about I was going to do this, or I was going to do that. Sometimes I can be a real dumb ass. But this much I know is true: Trust is either total, or it is non-existent, and commitment is absolute or not at all.

The rashes are getting very bad. I have not yet taken my drugs for the night either. I am getting tired of talking this bullshit. It is time to get into action.

I ate a hamburger for supper. I hate eating flesh. It doesn't make sense to eat that stuff. Anyway, if you do not have trust and commitment, you don't have anything at all.

We only have to ask one question of the person we would know. Would I be willing to go into combat with this person? If not, screw them. We do not have time to wait on the weak.

- Be strong.
- Be vigilant.
- Be brave.
- Be true.
- That is how I feel tonight.

If you walk behind me one day in the bush and do not cut and run, then you can be my friend. But even then, if at some later date you break. Screw you too. You do not deserve to live. And I will soon forget your name.

- God is strong.
- God is good.
- God gives life.
- God takes life.
- God is predictable.
- God is always there.
- God is dependable.
- God is strong.
- God is good.
- God gives life.
- God takes life.

Thursday, May 8, 1997

Well, I asked Mark to leave this afternoon. He was the last one. Now they are all gone, except me. I am here. Here in my little bunker with my guns and Buddha's. Guess it is not very funny anymore. It is rapidly ending, or is it coming to a new beginning?

This pen sucks!

The words are all gone. I have nothing left to say at AA meetings or to people. It is done, finis! Now we just wait. Sit on the cushion be quiet and wait. I need to switch sleeping habits, stay up all night, sleep during daylight, get ready, no food, no sleep, no people and feel nothing.

Thursday, May 22, 1997

I spent one more night at the Buddhist Temple. Mark is back. He came home and said, "Dad, do not ask me to leave again because I am not going. I am not going to leave you alone." That boy said he would be with me until the end. I thank God for him. We are going to go golfing today. I have lost over twenty-five pounds. Every day is clearer now. I have a three-day weekend. Soon we will know.

Three days no meat. Everything will be okay now. It is good. It is as it should be. I will be okay. I only have a few more days to prepare physically, mentally and emotionally. It will be as it should be.

I am cutting my meds back by 50% today. I must have total ability to function. The mind must be clear as fresh mountain air. Feel like singing to the loons on my Minnesota pond. Walk barefoot in the damp green grass. Body feels light. Eyes have regained the sparkle.

Michael, you must rest now. Find peace in your inner mind-fullness. Only we know our answers. Look within to find your own Peace Profound.

We are dying so "follow your own path."

Life is too brief. Half will be doing this - The other half will be doing that.

Monday, May 26, 1997

Everything is the same. It has been another week of separation with no contact. I do not know if it is getting harder or easier, but it is messed up for sure. I have not talked much about *she* for a while; it is still too painful.

I have a lot of hurt and anger. Tonight I am alone as I have been for at least thirty years. Even as a young child in northern Minnesota, I spent most of my time alone in the woods with my dog. Mine has been a life of little joy and much pain.

Yes, I wander from day to day doing those few structured things that give a false sense of stability, but I have no happiness, no joy, and little contentment. It is how it has always been. Moreover, one day they will bury this body, say a few kind words and forget about this pimple of existence.

Perhaps Pat will recall the time an AA guy with the same birthday bought him a meal of rice and chicken, but the memory will be brief, fleeting, and irrelevant to the movement. Some people have a cause or a purpose. When they leave they leave a page of recall. Perhaps Ho Chi Minh was one of those people. He struggled, suffered, and died. He did so because he believed in nationalism. He believed in freeing his people from French and American oppression. Mary said to me yesterday, "Dad just because you killed Vietnamese doesn't mean that you have to become one to get forgiveness." She is a very wise person, and I love her more than I can allow. Feel sad tonight about my life. Had dinner with the kids yesterday and left right after we ate. It hurts too much to be close to them right now. Maybe that's the way it has always been.

The great provider the emotionless provider. Big deal! They needed a father more than a source of income. But I did not know how to be one. I guess. Forgive me, my children.

May 28, 1997

Well, it is another day. I am trying to decide what it is that I want out of life. It seems like there are few choices.

1. Do I want a divorce?
2. Where do I want to live?
3. What do I want to do about work?

So far I have been delaying the answers to these questions. Mainly because *she* does not know what *she* wants.

I saw Dr. Lois yesterday. She asked me the following question, "If you set all the financial concerns aside, would you want to be with Donna?" My answer yesterday was, "No, probably not." But if I'm not with her then who am I? What will I do? Where will I go? The truth is that not much will change. We both will be okay financially, and we will still have our children. *She* will have her life and career, and I will have mine.

Saturday, May 31, 1997

Two days ago, I filled out the divorce papers. They are supposed to be ready today for Donna to read and sign. We could be divorced in four weeks. We had lunch on Wednesday. She was in a bad place. She said that I had never cared about her, said I was callous and said that she has been depressed and isolated. Said she was under a great deal of stress on her job.

I later called and suggested we try to work it out, and she should come home. She said she still had too many doubts. So, Thursday I called her and discussed terms of a divorce settlement and went to see a lawyer. I felt crappy about the whole thing, but I need some sort of closure on this situation.

Robert has two jobs for me in Kansas City, and my boss has one. I may have a job in Vietnam too. I have to move on with my life.

I realized this week that if we got back together, we would be harming each other more. We had roles that worked for many years, but they no longer work. Donna has changed, and I have changed. That is all I have for now.

Thursday, June 19, 1997

It has been a while since I wrote. A lot has happened in the past two weeks. Donna refused to sign the papers, so I finally threw up my hands and said, "Screw it!" I will do what I need to do until she makes up her mind and that will not be until the end of August.

I was finally at a breaking point. I was suicidal and homicidal. I realized that I needed to get out of Las Vegas. I took some time off from work and caught a plane to Minneapolis. I arrived sometime around noon and was totally stressed to the max. I don't think I planned to do anything crazy because when I landed, I went by and visited our old house in south Minneapolis. I then drove over to the Midway AA Club and was thinking about going to a meeting.

There might have been a couple of people at the club, but I do not remember speaking with anyone. I stayed a few minutes and had a cup of coffee. I decided my AA friend Larry lived nearby so I would go over and see him. When I got there, I was desperate to talk to someone. I pounded on his door and called out his name. I heard him yell from the inside, "Come back later." I turned and walked back to the car. That was it. Even Larry didn't have time to talk.

It was getting dark when I got to the massage parlor on Lake Street across from the White Castle. It was near where I used to work, and we lived as a family. I went into the massage parlor thinking I would get a massage and maybe relax. I was planning to spend the night in Minneapolis and then drive to my land the next day or go up and meet Sonny. I am not sure if I knew what I was going to do.

After the massage, I got up and walked out the door. There was a bar across the street. I was feeling physically and emotionally drained. I sat at the bar for a few minutes and thought about what I was about to do. I remember thinking, "I have been listening to teachers and preachers my whole life, now I am going to do what I want to do." So, after eighteen years and ten months of sobriety,

I started drinking again. That was on June 19[th,] and I have been drinking every day since. It is what it is and nothing more.

****

Today I sit in the trailer house on my Minnesota land. I have been drunk here for nearly two weeks. My brother Sonny is here with me. I have ranted and raved in a drunken stupor for the past two weeks. I am spewing up all that has happened in my life since January. We have gone golfing and fishing a few times, but I cannot get away from king alcohol. My brother is the only person left that I can trust.

Sunday I go home for a week of work. The following week I leave for three weeks in Vietnam. The last mission of resolution. If I return, I will have many decisions to make. However, the path will be clear. As of this writing, my thought is that I may not make it back from Vietnam this time. The truth is I am going there to die!

RETURN TO VIETNAM

If I make my bed in Hell, You are there.

—Psalm 139:8 (NKJV)

Friday, July 5, 1997

I've been in Bien Hoa two days. Unbelievable. I am really screwed up. I drank snake whiskey last night with an old woman from Hanoi and lost my jade ring and $50.

I do not know what the hell I'm doing here. Maybe go to Vung Tau in the morning. Sixteen hours to fly here. No Americans here - all NVA. Only one here - by myself. Stink of snake whiskey and nuoc mam.

Wednesday, July 10, 1997

Been a special guest of the Communist Party Republic of Vietnam for past several days. Mr. H. is special tour guide for me. Saw many beautiful places and take a crazy bus ride from Bien Hoa: Song Dong Nai as it is now known.

Swimming in South China Sea very good for my spirit. Been feeling very sad since I go to Vung Tau, Vietnam.

Yesterday went on a long walk to beach and sat by Quac Te; the monument to soldiers who died for freedom and reunification of Vietnam.

Yesterday meet with eighty-five-year-old monk. Talk with him about Buddha.

Yesterday, special guest for lunch with mother who helps all people. She feed students at hotel school and help everybody. Saw crazy fool on one of my walks. He was yelling at me while I drink coffee. He smash big rock into bicycle, and he throw food at street in front of me. Then he dropped his pants at me; front and back! One Vietnamese he start beating him with club and finally tie him up with rope.

Three times yesterday, I have much internal fear. Last night I sat in front of hotel school talk to students in English. Later I was special guest of member of board of directors for tourist school and Communist party member.

He said all American soldiers like Vietnamese soup and Vietnamese women. He had very much to drink. He insisted I drink with him and eat Hanoi soup. He name Mr. Nguyen.

Thursday, July 11, 1997

Went to Saigon and spent several days drinking in Backpacker, Disco and Apocalypse Now bars. Met several veterans including Russell. He was with the First Cav at the Ia Drang Valley battle. He and his wife live in a hotel. He has been there eight years or so. Seems to be connected with the American ambassador and several missing in action (MIA) groups.

After a few days, I left for Da Lat, a city in the central highlands with a lady I met at the Back Packer bar. Her name is Linh. Spent three days there and saw everything there was to see on a motorcycle. Very fun trip. Beautiful place with a lot of trees and mountains. It has a lake in the middle of town. Nice place to take a ride on a horse-drawn cart.

From there back to Saigon, now called Ho Chi Minh City. Spent a few days there and left for the Mekong Delta by bus. Ten hours of bus ride. From there took boat up the river for several hours near the Cambodia border.

Met many family members during this trip. Mother, stepfather, (Former VC) and foster mother and foster father. Brothers and sisters were also there. Very rewarding time in the delta. Nice place to visit and maybe someday live.

Returned to the USA on July 27th.

VA PSYCHIATRIC WARD CONFINEMENT #2

Tuesday, August 5, 1997

This is a quick update. I started drinking on the 19th of June. I spent a couple of weeks in Minnesota with Sonny. I went to Vietnam on the 2nd of July and came home on the 27th. I was in really bad shape when I got home and had to spend five days in VA psych ward. I don't remember much about it. I have been sober for eight days. I would have had 19 years of sobriety in nine days. Donna came back to the house last Saturday. I had my meeting with the VA review board this morning for an increase in PTSD rating. I am 60% for cancer and 10% for PTSD. Don't know where I am going right now. I am just taking it one day at a time. I am having trouble getting back to AA, but do not want to drink anymore. It is a dead end street for me. Flashbacks and panic attacks are increasing. I had a bad one during the review meeting this morning. I am still shaking from its impact. I don't know where I want to be. It is very difficult and quite sad. I haven't been able to work in months. The job has been hard since we lost the contract and with all the changes at the company. I don't know. I just don't know right now.

Hotel California keeps going through my mind. Riverboats up the Mekong River into Cambodia. I keep thinking about the road trips to Da Lat, Vung Tau, Chau Doc, and wherever else. Bus rides for ten hours and motorcycle rides from Bien Hoa to God knows where, and horseback, bicycle, and taxi. And God knows what else happened over there.

Friday, August 8, 1997

It is one more day in the life of this Vietnam veteran. Donna and I went to dinner last night and talked. I told her that I was still planning to go back to Vietnam and teach. She did not like it but agreed that she would be okay. We can stay married and see how it goes. I will have to take early retirement from my job. They are supposed to be offering an early retirement package this month or next. I told her I would be accepting the package. That combined with a disability increase should allow us to be able to do it financially.

Monday, August 11, 1997

I got drunk Saturday night and stayed downtown all night drinking. I came home about six in the morning. Donna was very upset, and so were the kids. I am not sure where to go from here. I seem to be unable to get off the alcohol.

I spoke with one of the guys I met in Vietnam. His name is Russell. He is coming to the states to spend some time in the VA to dry out. He said he would call me when he gets back to the states. He told me that Linh was waiting to see me again. She is waiting to see me in Vietnam, and my wife here is waiting for me to leave. I guess I need to make the tough decisions.

Tuesday, August 12, 1997

It is one more day in the life of a sick human. Donna is still upset. She left me a note yesterday telling me to get some help. She also said she is here and never really left. It may seem that way to her but not to me. When she left everything changed.

Today, I will do what I need and want to do. My whole life I have been doing what others expect of me. First I listened to brother and mother, then preachers and teachers, then officers and boss, then wife and family. Today I know my life is brief and I will do what I need to do to keep my heart alive. Not dead.

Much has happened these past few months. Yes, I am drinking, but I have also lived a lot in the past few months. We must follow our own path now before it is too late. I spent many hours on the bus and on the boat and had time to think about my life.

From Vung Tau to Da Lat to the Mekong Delta, I think, I look, I wait, and I learn. No, I was not drunk all the time in Vietnam. Most of the time that I was there, I was sober and totally alive.

I have scheduled another trip to Vietnam on August 30 and will return in two weeks. This time I will come back with a job and retire January 1st

And return to live and work in Vietnam. This I know for sure.

Thursday, August 14, 1997

Today is my dead mother's birthday and would have been my nineteenth year of sobriety. Well, Donna is pissed off this morning. I let her listen to a message from a corporate guy in Singapore that said I was moving to Vietnam. I think it finally hit her that I am indeed going and probably will be gone long term.

Apparently, that company is looking for something for me to do until the office opens in Saigon. I would like to have the country manager's job in that office when it opens. To be honest about it I have dreamt about being a Southeast Asian country manager for a very long time. However, I did not plan on doing it drunk.

Dr. Nancy gave me a stern lecture Tuesday about what I should be doing with my life. Screw it. I am a free spirit now. It started the day Donna, and I separated. No more will I live my life for anyone else.

Monday, August 18, 1997

I spent last weekend in Los Angles. I went down there to visit the Lee family. I stayed drunk in a dirty hotel room by myself most of the time. I really had a great time. (ha-ha)

I am still somewhat confused about my life. I plan to retire at about $3,000 per month, move to Vietnam, and work for an American communications company, teach English, or work for someone else.

I am leaving for Vietnam on August 30, 1997, to firm up some sort of job. I am meeting with Hong's brother in Saigon. He runs a watch store in the Saigon mall. The song, "Don't cry for me Argentina." keeps repeating itself in my head.

This week I need to start pushing from top to bottom. I am going to call our company senior executives today and request their help in securing a job in Asia.

Tuesday, August 19, 1997

It is morning, and the sun is just coming up. Our granddaughter woke us up at five this morning. I am still sleeping in my private room on the floor. Donna is patient about it all.

I met with Dr. Nancy yesterday. She still thinks I am making too many decisions at a bad time in my life. She believes it is being driven by PTSD and alcoholism. I said, "I don't know." a lot yesterday. I am trying to be as objective as I can about what is going on. So let me set down the truth as best I can.

I want to go to Vietnam because I feel needed and useful and I can do whatever I want while I am there. I no longer feel connected here. It is my own choice to go.

The obsessive behavior for guns has lessened, and I do not feel self-destructive. I think about going back every day. Can I set these next things in print? I am not sure, but I need to try. My armpits are sweating right now; water is running down the side of my chest.

I met an Amerasian woman while I was in Vietnam. She is a taxi girl. In other words, she has sex with people for a living. I spent a couple of weeks traveling with her. I met her mother and stepfather. I met her foster parents and her son. She was married for a few years to a Vietnamese man. She smokes, drinks, and cusses. Her teeth are a dark brown and full of cavities. She cannot read or write but is one of the toughest people I have ever met.

I did not sleep with her, but she made me feel like a man again. We had a great adventure. We went to Da Lat up in the mountains in the central highlands and traveled all over the Mekong Delta. She is from a little village called Can Tho. We went by boat, motorcycle, and bus. Sweat is pouring from my armpits now. I am getting honest in this journal.

Her heart is dead except when she is with her son; then she

becomes someone else. Her life mission is to focus on him and provide for him. She took care of me while I was there and protected me from the demon alcohol. She touched my heart in a different way. Now my mind and my heart are both in Vietnam, but not because of Linh. I don't believe we could ever have a meaningful relationship. My heart is in Vietnam because of the people of Vietnam.

Many people believed my obsession with the country was because of the lady I met in 1967. Now I know it is not so. When I am there, I feel needed, unique, important, and useful. I love the country, the language, and the people. I am old enough to know there are bad people everywhere. I know the games, the cons, and the bull-shit. And there is plenty of that in Vietnam and in the USA.

Now the dilemma is this. What do I do about my life here? What do I do about my wife, children and thirty years of living here? Do I need to let it go to be there, or can I somehow do both? And if I do both, can I be true to both? And if I don't do both, who do I hurt?

In life, many people are called, but few are selected. Time gets shorter by the day. If we don't do it now, when will we do it? Donna kissed me goodbye a little while ago. I think she still cares. I do not want to hurt her anymore, but I know that we can no longer be together.

The words from the lady at the hotel in Vung Tau keep coming back to me. "Mr. Hein is a very poor man, but he is a good man." My question to her was, "If Mr. Hein was a very rich man could he still be a good man?" After a long pause, she said, "No I don't think so." Money corrupts. Material objects can deaden the heart and kill the soul. Life is so simple alone in the woods. Water is running from my armpits again.

I am not sure what else to say. I have been speaking with Russell from Vietnam. He is back at his wife's house. She served him divorce papers a week before he came back. He is faced with the same questions that I am.

Ed said he lives his life by meandering from place to place on the planet earth. He has been doing that since his wife left him ten years ago. He has found peace in Vietnam. I do not know if I will find peace there, but maybe.

I only know this. When I was there, I didn't want to come back, and when I am here, I am obsessed with going back. And I believe that is no reflection on what I have here. It is much deeper. It has been with me since I was a child when I used to draw pictures of Asian people. Vietnam has always been part of who I am.

Perhaps I will end up serving Buddha in some monastery near the Cambodian border. I don't know.

Peace and love brother Sonny, the one that knows all, and still loves me. Thank you for your love brother.

Wednesday, August 27, 1997

I am feeling sad this morning. Maybe it is because I got drunk last night, and did not take my medications. Donna has been easy to be with the last couple of weeks. That makes it more difficult to leave this Saturday.

Not sure what the hell is going on. The longer I am here, the less I want to leave. But I know I must leave and do this thing.

I had a tough session with Dr. Nancy on Monday. She is concerned that all of my decisions might be the result of PTSD and my desire to destroy myself. Truth is I am not sure what is driving my decisions.

I feel no remorse about the drinking, or the attitude, or anything else for that matter. Dr. Nancy said the change started when I took back control over my life while Donna was gone. I am still in charge, and boy am I ever in charge. I feel some anger right now.

I am supposed to meet the communication company guy in Singapore while I am there. I hope I get the job. That would be good; otherwise, I am not sure how I will make it on just my half of my pension. I need to call my current boss and talk to him about the trip. Maybe he would pick up my travel expenses.

SECOND TRIP
BACK TO VIETNAM

Let not you become teachers for we all stumble in many things.

—James 3:1-2 (NKJV)

Monday, September 15, 1997

I made it back from the swamp one more time. I got back yesterday afternoon. I spent two weeks looking for work in Saigon. If I want it, I have a job teaching English at a foreign language institute starting in January. In fact, I have ordered my six-month teaching visa. It cost $200.

These past two weeks were quite different from July. I guess Vietnam has taken on a more realistic look this time. To be honest, it is a sorry place to live. It is hot, humid, and the people are only after your money. The country has no morals or values; everyone is out to con the next man down the road.

I am still talking to the communications company about opening an office in Saigon, now called Ho Chi Minh City (HCMC) by the Communist government. I also have a possible job with another company, and I may have an opportunity with still a third organization. I will be meeting with their vice president, on the 29th. Overall, it was a bit of a costly trip. I didn't drink much. I gave out a lot of resumes and hung out in the hotel room with Linh.

I saw a little old naked man squatting on the street. He was naked except for the red shorts that were around his ankles. There were people everywhere. He was squatted and turning around in circles while he was trying to dig a huge turd out of his ass with a stick. Either it was a turd, or maybe it was his guts. Whatever, the scene painted an appropriate picture of Vietnam in my mind's eye.

Linh brought me to visit an old woman monk near the airport. She chanted for me and removed a thirty-year curse. She said:

1. I was a Buddha in a prior life.
2. I have died three times in this life.
3. Two dead Vietnamese have been chasing me.
4. She redirected them to chase the Buddha instead of me.
5. She said the nightmares would be removed forever.
6. I had to eat Chinese paper with characters written in chicken blood for three days.
7. I have to continue to chant a daily Buddhist mantra.

The faces were the same but more recognizable this trip. I taught school for a few hours. That would not be an easy occupation for $10 bucks an hour. Today, I think I will return to Vietnam only if I have a better job than teaching English.

For $400, I rented a house for three months in case I need a place to stay. Linh will be living there until I return. I feel confused today. I am still on Vietnam time. It will take a few days to adjust. Donna still thinks I am crazy and wants me to get treatment. I will wait a few days until my head clears some. I gave Russell $852 to get his ass back to the swamp. The bastard had better return the favor when I need it. Bloody hell, I feel tired and off balance today.

Tuesday, September 16, 1997

I have always sought to tell the truth. Yet today I cannot talk, nor can I even write about what is going on. Perhaps it is the fear of seeing the insanity in black and white.

Donna broke into my bedroom bunker while I was gone and took all my guns and knives, and put a bed in place of my sleeping bag. I told her this morning it feels like I have been castrated and that she reinforces the idea that I am crazy.

If I am crazy, or PTSD crazed, or alcoholic, then everything makes sense to her. However, if I am rational and sane, then none of my behavior makes sense to her. What is my behavior exactly?

I am getting ready to give up a $100k a year job to move to a crappy country to teach English to a bunch of communists for $10 per hour. If only viewed from this perspective it does not make much sense. But like Plato's white elephant; they can only see the leg, and it feels like a tree. The truth of my insanity is this. I have paid six months' rent on a two-story house for a prostitute and her son. I can live there when I return. For whatever reason, I feel needed there and not needed here. What I have here is dead.

The lady's name is Linh, and she sells her body to support herself and her son. She has been doing that for three years. She is Amerasian, which means she is half-American and half Vietnamese. She cannot read or write and only has one year of school. She is twenty-nine years old. She doesn't know what her American father's name is or exactly when she was born. She has lived on her own since the age of eleven. She is a street person, tough, she smokes and drinks and likes to disco. She also picks her nose and farts in public.

I traveled with her during my July trip. We did not sleep together. We only traveled together. She never asked for money, and I didn't offer any. I met her mother, stepfather, son, and second family. We had many long trips on boats and buses. I was speaking Vietnamese and broken English and eating nuoc mam and rice. My heart was dead when I left Las Vegas, and it began coming to life in Vietnam.

This trip was business. Linh speaks the truth, or so it seems. There was little drinking, no disco, no bars, only talks and time together. She now has her son with her and a house. However, I think she will continue to work the streets when she needs money.

Mr. Hai tried to give me his nineteen-year-old daughter when I return to Vietnam. His only stipulation was that I send her to school, and if I did that, she could be my slave. I turned him down, but what kind of culture would have a man even offer his child like that.

I have a separate account with Schwab and a credit card in my name. I have opened an account with a Hong Kong Bank in Vietnam. I know I can live there and be taken care of by many people. I can live there at least until the money is gone.

My impotence caused by prostate cancer surgery is a struggle. I cannot make love to a woman. Linh understands this, but she is young and will leave me for another man. Like Donna did. So I live alone here or there. It is the same.

Teaching or any kind of work is difficult for me now. I sweat, shake, and hyperventilate. I only had one flashback and panic attack in Vietnam on this trip. Do not ever reject me!

I am alone but cannot deal with being alone. I cannot be touched but crave contact. I need to be hugged, and held, and cared for, but I will not let anybody touch my body. I want to cry and be angry, but I feel nothing.

I had heavy sweats last night. Is that physical or mental? Something is trying to work its way out of my flesh.

Take my guns, take my knives, let my blood flow in your room, but always remember this: I will not die! Shave my head! Send me to Vietnam to kill the yellow man! But I will not die! Cut my flesh! Stop my breath! But I will not die!

For my death occurred in the month of July in the year 1967, and because of this, no man can kill me again. Ever!

Monday, September 22, 1997

Tonight I am in Atlanta for a few days of computer training. I went out and got smashed last Saturday night and ended up in a bar throwing up and passed out in the car. I was definitely in a blackout. I may have to give up alcohol before it kills me.

I am feeling a little confused about where I am going from here. Right now, I guess I will leave it up to fate. If I get one of the good jobs, I will definitely go over to the swamp. I may still go even if I have to teach English. I do not know. I have several difficult decisions coming up in the next couple of months.

I signed up for penile implant surgery next Monday. I have some apprehension about it, but it is one of those things I need to have done while I am still working and have insurance. The other things, like divorce, may have to wait until next year. If Donna and I can make it that long, she is angry about my lack of participation.

I have cut way back on the anti-anxiety drugs, and I feel better. I feel less anxious when I do not take the anxiety medications. I have not had flashbacks or panic attacks for a while. I guess the last one I had was in the hotel in Saigon. I had a bad one there. I am scared about possibilities of rejection and will not tolerate any more rejection. I will live alone before that happens.

I am studying Vietnamese daily. I guess that means the obsession has not yet left me. Huh? It is awfully quiet in this hotel room. It seems like this silence is tearing at my brain. I have too much time to think. I need to talk to someone, get drunk, or something. I hate having quiet time alone. That must mean something.

At some point, I need to look at my life rationally. Dr. Nancy asked me where I wanted to be in five or ten years. That really blew me away. I have not thought about any future for a long time. What is my vision now? Where do I want to be in five years? Beats the hell out of me!

Right now, I have no long-range plans. I am only thinking about the next couple of months, and I feel sad even thinking about that. I feel like I am on the river headed downstream again and can't get off the damn log if you know what I mean? But, I do have choices. Don't I? I can choose to leave or decide to stay. I can choose to drink or choose not to drink. I can choose to retire or choose not to. These are the choices. Aren't they? And yet, what is this powerful pull that keeps drawing me back to the abyss? Why would anyone want to go to Vietnam to live or die?

Sitting here tonight I see my face in the mirror, and I don't know this face anymore. He is not the one that used to be under this flesh. Someone else is here now. He is a stranger to me, and yet somehow, I know his name and his place, and now it is his time. These things I know. He is in the glass, and someone is talking to him about me, and about what he ought to be doing with this flesh, and when it should live, and when it should die, and where it should live, and where it should die. He knows these things better than I do for he has been with me longer than I have. He was here before the flesh and will be here after the flesh has decayed. He was a monk, a master, a child, an old man, a bird, a stone, and a dog. He lives by a different law; an older law. The law that is based on what was, and not what is.

Friday, September 26, 1997

I have one more day in this sack of flesh. I had two bad days in Atlanta. I drank all night Wednesday. I have got to give it up. The alcohol is getting progressively worse every time. It is hard but I know I must quit now. No matter what I end up doing or where I end up going, I must not drink.

I spoke to Linh this morning. I had Russell check out some things for me. I guess it is okay. I am feeling alone today. Donna and Martha are gone for the week. I go into the hospital for the surgery next Monday. I am going to get a new pump penis. Several people have told me I am crazy, but it is something I must do to regain my manhood.

Maybe I need to go back to AA or find some kind of spiritual help. Maybe Buddha can help with the alcohol. I do not know right now, but I must give it up. I feel displaced this morning. Maybe I need to take my medications.

Goodbye for now journal.

Sunday, September 28, 1997

I just got off the phone with a friend. He told me he and his family moved to Louisiana. We talked some about my situation. This is the toughest place I have ever been. I have always been one hundred percent honest with people around me. Now I find myself in a position where it is to my benefit not to reveal everything. I do not like being on the emotional fence. I would feel a hell of a lot better if I could be honest with everyone.

The truth is I will be going back to Vietnam in January for several reasons some of which follow:

- I feel emotionally connected to Linh.
- I feel needed there.
- It is exciting to be there.
- I feel special and unique over there.
- The language is fun.
- I feel important there.
- It is thrilling to ride bikes there.
- I crave understanding of the people.
- I am never alone there.
- I feel like a man when I am over there.

Now, are these sufficient reasons to give up a $160k per year job, a wife of twenty-six years, stability, financial security, and perhaps my country? Tonight I think so. Tonight I feel like I belong in Vietnam. If I could get on a plane, I would leave this minute.

I still have no negative feelings for Donna. Our life together was good, but it is different now and, I am convinced, it can never be what it was. So, what do I do? Do I tell her about Linh? File for divorce? Sell the house? Split our assets? Should I just pack up and walk out the door? Should I walk out the door and then turn out the lights?

I have thought about returning to Vietnam for thirty years. I returned, and now I cannot stay away. It is not the woman. It is the thrill of it all and the challenge. I am meeting new people every day; some are good, and many are bad. It is the trying to get inside their brain that makes it challenging. To become more Vietnamese than they are. I look forward to absorbing myself in the mystery of it all; maybe to shave my head and be a monk for a while. I do not know. Maybe I will make a difference in a few people's life before I die. The ones we left behind, the re-education camp people that live on the streets. Maybe that is it. Maybe there is someone over there that needs my return. I do not know if writing about it has helped much. It seems like what is required of me now is to get honest.

In the morning, I go under the knife again. I am scared about that. I will have to take care of myself after the surgery. I keep thinking it might be a mistake. Donna thinks it is, and so does Linh. But then Linh said if I do it, do it for myself; and that is why I am going in at 6:00 am to have it done. After the procedure is finished, I must get on with the other things I need to do. I have three months to take care of this stuff. I must have the courage to act soon. For me, it has never worked to hedge my bets. I am what I am, and I am doing what I am doing, and that is just the way it is.

Monday, October 6, 1997

The last time I wrote I was in a bit of a quandary about what to do. Well since then I have done quite a lot. Donna signed the divorce papers. I met with my Vietnam Special Forces man, Joe, at the club last week and he convinced me that I needed to get off the fence and make a decision for my sake and the families. He said that if I don't, I could get filed against while I am over in Vietnam and end up losing a lot more because it would be sent to my last known address and I could not respond within the proper time.

So, I talked with Donna, and she agreed to sign after some

pretty dramatic changes in the original offer. She will get the house, cars, no debt on the cars, half my 401k, half my retirement, and $500 per month for child support. I get the land, all my guns and ammo, half my retirement check, half my 401k, and my freedom. It is not bad I guess. She needs to go to a class, and I need to file with the court. Two weeks later, we will have the divorce. As it stands now, I will stay here until January. That is it for now journal.

October 9, 1997

Tonight Donna is going to the class, and after that, it will all start. In two weeks, we will have the divorce. It is easy to get divorced in Las Vegas. I am not sure how I feel about all that, but it will happen now. I am still feeling some pain over the surgery, but the swelling has gone down. It will allow me to screw my way through Asia if I so choose. Guess I have become a self-centered son of a bitch. Oh well, what is… is.

My boss spent the week out here. We entertained customers all week with golf and dinners. There isn't much happening on the job front. I am concerned about how I will make it on my limited retirement income since I have to pay off the car and give Donna child support and half my retirement. I can make it if I do not have a house or a car, and if I only eat rice and fish. So, that is it for now.

Bye.

Friday, October 17, 1997

Well, it is about over now. Two more weeks and the divorce will be final. I am starting to wonder some about it all. Where will I be five years from now?

I still have to work out a job and figure out how much money I will be making if I don't have a job. It seems strange that I will be homeless in a few weeks. I will have no car and little money. I guess I have been spoiled over the past many years.

I do not want to end up like my stepdad or a few other people I know. I do not want to end up living in a trailer house on my land, alone with my booze and guns. Right now that doesn't sound too good to me. Maybe it will sound good after a year in Vietnam.

No goals, no striving, no achieving, no struggle. It all sounds scary to me today. Susan is in town. I will be seeing her later today. I am looking forward to that. I will probably get drunk and spend the night downtown. Next week I go to Florida for one week. I just got a fax coming in; I feel a little nervous about getting faxes sent here.

Russell wants me to call his daughter and ask for more money. Oh well, who knows where we are going.

Goodbye for now.

Tuesday, October 21, 1997

I am staying at the Swan hotel in Orlando for training. I am trying to move the corporate political machine, but so far, it is going slowly. I made a proposal to a supervisor to work for his team in Asia. He expressed some interest, but that is about it. I have made up my mind that I am out of here. I am ready to take my life into my own hands.

That is it for now.

Wednesday, October 23, 1997

Today I am having a great day. I met with the people from Singapore. They want to hire me for a job in Saigon. I am really messed up from drinking right now. I just talked to my friend Russell in Vietnam. Told him to get my friend Linh on the phone. Now!

I was drinking all night. Very sad but ready to go… so here I go. I am having trouble spelling these words right now… Very drunk…

So I will talk to my friend Linh and be okay for the night. God Bless.

Sunday, October 26, 1997

I am still in Orlando. I think I am finally going home today. Well, I say I am going home; it is no longer my home. Only a place I call home for the time being. We got our divorce decree in the mail on Friday. Signed, sealed, and delivered. I feel weird about it all. It looks like I got the job in Vietnam. However, I have lost a lot in the process.

I guess weird is not the right word. Perhaps sad would be more appropriate. It is indeed a strange life. We know not where it is taking us. Guess that is all for now.

Monday, November 3, 1997

I am still feeling a lot of fear and discomfort, especially about retirement. Retirement after twenty-eight years is a major decision. Economic fear has always been one of my biggest fears.

My drinking is continuing to get worse. I got drunk last Thursday and stayed downtown gambling all night. I had a lot of trouble driving home in the morning. I had planned to go to LA but didn't make it. I was drinking Jack Daniel's and coke most of the night. That crap gives me a bad hangover. The dog is downstairs barking, and it is only six in the morning.

I am quite stable as far as Vietnam goes. However, I have too much other stuff on my mind to be crazy. Stuff like; will I have a job soon? I still have not heard from the boys in Singapore; I am having a lot of apprehension about that. I badly need a job, and I don't think working as an English teacher in Vietnam will get it.

In fact, I don't know what I would do if I have to get up and go to work on a regular basis; it might kill me. The damn dog is barking again. I tried to call Jimmy A. yesterday. There wasn't an answering machine on the line and no answer. I will have to try to reach him at work today.

My sales job is pretty much dead. I do not know what to say to customers whom I have not seen in several weeks. I should get my retirement package this week. I will sign it and get on with it. My life feels pretty screwed up right now. I am beginning to think of the impact of leaving my family, job, and not having a plan for the future. I have had a stable life for a long time. It's hard to ignore the entirety of my life. It is as if I am shutting the door and turning out the lights in my life.

I need to remember that all I have is this one day and I can hack anything for this one day. I will be okay even if the phone no longer rings with customer calls, but I do not know if I will be okay not seeing my kids.

I need to get up and do a voucher. I downloaded maps of Laos and Cambodia this morning. The sun is shining in my window; the dog quit barking; I am leaving; don't know where I am going; don't know when I will return.

Tuesday, November 4, 1997

I feel good today because I got a call from Singapore last night. They said that I would be getting a "package" from them within the next few days. Wow! I may, in fact, have the job of my dreams. I will be a communication company country manager for Vietnam, Cambodia, and Laos. What a choice deal. I am so excited. I am ready to go and get started.

Tuesday, November 18, 1997

I am back at work. Yesterday I signed my retirement papers and mailed them in. Last week Donna and I spent the week with Sonny. His son Ed was killed in a car accident. Not much to say except it will be damn tough on Sonny and Betsy.

I had one bad night in Minnesota drinking at the funeral. It seems like it is at least once a week with an all-night drunk.

I am still waiting on a package from Singapore. I called again last night. They left a message that I should get a package by Monday or Tuesday of next week. Not much else to say.

I spoke to Russell last night. He is in New Jersey staying with his brother. Said he would be going back to Nam with me in January. I need to decide what to do with these people in Vietnam.

I also left a message for Miss Hang about my visa. I need to keep moving forward toward that day. Donna gave me a shot of guilt last night with a comment about "How does it feel to be running away from all of this?" I didn't have a really good answer.

I just know it is something I have to do. We will see how it turns out in the long run. If I get this good job, I could make a lot of money over the next few years. I think that is what will happen, but I could be wrong; I could end up a dead drunk in the streets of Saigon. We will see.

Monday, December 1, 1997

I am getting really bad with the drinking. I had another rough weekend. I got drunk and left a guy downtown and came home and raised hell here at home. I was banging on doors and yelling crazy stuff. I will have to give it up again. It is not an easy thing to do; however, especially with my life in the mess, it is in right now.

I told Donna I would check into this alcohol weekend workshop thing today. Maybe that would help. I still have not received a package from my friends in Singapore, and I am getting tired of waiting.

If I cannot get into the alcohol workshop, I may stay with the monk for a few days away from everything and see if that helps. We will see. I am going to Kansas City next week for a company class and staff meeting. Oh, I rented a secure storage place for my guns, ammo, knives, and personal goods. That's it for now.

Tuesday, December 2, 1997

I feel a little better today. I spent some time with Chaiya yesterday. We talked about my need to stay off alcohol. I also quit chewing snuff yesterday. I meditated last night and this morning. I am still feeling shaky, but a little better.

My boss just called and said they were giving me an extra $4,000 because I'm such a hard worker. That means I should get $9,500 in December for a Christmas bonus. That should be just about enough to pay off Donna's car.

I have been up since 4:00 am, and I am feeling tired. Oh, I didn't have any coffee this morning either. That is what you call a major change.

Saturday, December 6, 1997

This week I received my job package. It is better than I could have imagined. They will pay me $6,000 per month. Plus $350 per month transportation allowance. That is $76,200 per year! Plus, vacation of fourteen days, medical coverage, all paid business expenses, office materials, and a one-year contract.

It is a thirty-year dream come true. They will handle visas and all business travel and expenses. Too, damn good to be true!

What more can I say? I am going to Kansas City for my retirement party and a class next week. I will write more when I get there.

Tuesday, December 9, 1997

I am in Kansas City, and I went out and had a few beers at the VFW last night. I got back to the hotel about four this morning. It was another short, drunk, night, but now I am done drinking for the week. Denny and I went to dinner last night.

I had my retirement get together today. My supervisor roasted me in front of the team. They gave me a nice travel bag, card, and a day timer. I went to dinner with the group tonight. I am tired, and it is getting late. I am going to bed. I will see Sara tomorrow night.

Monday, December 22, 1997

I am waiting for my new company to send me the contract and my work permit. I am leaving in only a few days. Mickey was in Las Vegas last week. He is going to pick up the Vegas job and handle it from Kansas City. I got drunk over the weekend again.

I had to turn in the car last week, and it was a good thing because at least I will not wreck it before I leave. I paid off Donna's car today. It cost me $11,991, so cash will be a little tight this Christmas, and I have bought no gifts. I am still waiting on a signed contract from my new company in Singapore.

King alcohol is kicking my ass. Obsession is getting worse by the day. I have very little short-term memory left. I talked to my AA sponsor Taft last week. He gave me some grief about drinking again. I told him I would quit when the consequences got bad enough. I wonder when that will be and how bad it will have to get. It is pretty bad right now.

Guess I am hoping the drinking will slow in Vietnam because I will be so busy. Truth is I doubt it, but I will need to quit at some point.

Friday, December 26, 1997

Christmas is over, and I wait to leave. I got my tickets this week and ordered my visa. Soon I will be on the plane. I still do not have a signed contract, but it doesn't matter I am going with or without it. The storage of my weapons is about done, and I have my land and some cash in a safe deposit box in Minnesota just in case.

MOVED TO VIETNAM

Tuesday, February 24, 1998

It has been a while since I last wrote in the journal. I have been in Vietnam since January 10th, and it has been crazy. I got the contract and spent a week in Singapore meeting my new team. I have already spent a week in Cambodia getting my work permit figured out.

I am living with Miss Linh at the house. It's been going okay, but I had to pay off the police to allow me to live with her. The communist government has a law that Vietnamese women cannot live with foreigners in this country. So, I can expect the secret police to be at the door once a month for tea and cash.

I have had some good days and some bad drinking days. One night I ended up at a hotel with two women. They ripped me off for $300 and my passport. Fortunately, the Vietnamese mafia sold the passport back to me a couple of days later for $130. Outside of those little adventures, I don't have much to report.

I went out last night with one of my channel partners and had several beers and dinner. We had a good time, and I went back to the house after dinner. Today I meet with a couple of other business partners for the first time.

Tuesday, February 24, 1998

I will be spending the night alone in this little place called a house. It is seven in the evening, and it is ninety degrees in here. We have no air conditioner, no shower, no hot water, and only a bucket pulled from a tub of water, called a cistern, for a bath. Not much else, a camping stove, a rice cooker, small icebox, a couple of fans and a bed. That is about it. Oh, I almost forgot; I have a chair and a small desk, that I call an office. But it is hot as hell in here!

Last weekend Linh and I went swimming in a hotel pool near here. That was fun, and we both got clean. The weekend, before last, we went to Tay Ninh and spent the day climbing a mountain to see a Buddhist Pagoda. That was a workout too.

My rashes are getting worse. I have them all over my ass and right arm. I tried some Vietnamese medicine, but it burned the skin on my arm, and the rashes seem to be growing around the burn.

Tomorrow I pick up my four-hundred dollar ring. I am having one made out of a one ounce, 24 karat, gold Chinese Panda coin that I had lying around.

I am feeling a little pensive tonight here alone. I do not like being alone. I have to prepare a report for Singapore sometime this week. Maybe I will get that started in the morning.

Monday, March 2, 1998

It is Monday and a new month in Vietnam. Not much happened this past weekend. It was quiet. Linh and I took a Honda for a ride in the streets of Ho Chi Minh for the first time yesterday. We sat on the banks of the Saigon River and watched the boats. It was a very relaxing time, and I was sober.

Linh's old boyfriend came back from Australia last week and is now living with Ms. Dao. I guess that is okay with me. What is... is.

I have my computer and cell phone so guess I am ready to get busy with selling stuff. One month has gone by already, and I have very little to show for my time on the job.

Friday, March 6, 1998

It is another day in the life of this wandering soul. Linh and I moved into a different house yesterday. It has a hose hanging from a shower faucet, two rooms up with air conditioners! What a relief to be able to sleep with air once again. It has been around ninety-three degrees at night here the past few weeks. And I have a spare bedroom for office space.

The job is going okay. I am still trying to get close to Ross, but that will take some time. He is a pretty amazing guy. He informed me yesterday that there is only one country manager per country and he is it for Vietnam. So I will change the title on my business cards to sales director. That is good enough for the first year anyway.

I guess Russell called for Phuoc yesterday and spoke with Tam instead. Tam told Russell that Phuoc has a new husband now. Life in Vietnam is stimulating to say the least.

My drinking recently has been contained to two or three large bottles of BGI per day. (BGI is a pilsner-type beer brewed in Tien Giang, Vietnam.) Seems to be working okay since the last binge which was a week or so ago. I am okay if I have three or fewer liters of BGI, any more and I am off and running with the vodka.

I am having drinking dreams lately, and I had one last night.

I dreamt I was wandering around in the U.S. drunk. I think it was Brother Chuck that picked me up at the last bar and took me home.

Monday, March 9, 1998

Well, I have something to write home about because I got drunk Saturday night here in HCMC. I told Dai, my security guy, to get a Honda and take me to Vung Tau. I drank all the way there. We arrived at midnight. We met a couple of trai-gai, gay boys, on the road. Dai got me there alive, and I ended up passing out in a shack on the beach.

The good news is I did not lose my passport, money, jewels or my life. The bad news is I did not bother telling Linh where I was going and she was up all night looking in HCMC bars for me. She was really upset.

I am going to buy some more jade in the morning. It seems like a lot of my money is going into jewelry. I have been studying Vietnamese for one hour per day this past week with a teacher at the house. I am starting out with the ABC's and moving forward from there. That has been rather enjoyable.

Monday, March 9, 1998

This morning I spoke with Donna. She is angry about the $30k she claims I wasted in company stock. She said I would have to pay thousands of dollars in taxes, but she has not spoken to an accountant yet. So, I guess we will wait and see.

It has been a bad day all around. Linh was crying at lunch, I guess over not having a family. This afternoon she asked me if I gave money to the woman she beat up for a lost chain. I told her that I did not. Everyone here would like to see us split up. They tell me she is messing around and tell her bull-shit about me messing around too.

It has been a bad day all around.

SECOND TRIP TO CAMBODIA

Wednesday, March 11, 1998

I am sitting at the HCMC airport waiting on Vietnam airlines to take me to Phnom Penh. The plane is going to be two hours late again. Isn't that the way it goes in Vietnam? I suppose it gives me a little time to ponder life anyway. I spoke with Donna twice this week. She seemed a little less tense the last time. Said she sent me a formal letter complaining about the taxes.

Linh is going to Can Tho for the next couple of days while I am in Cambodia. I think she is going to bring her son back with her. I will probably have to hire a maid to take care of the child. Oh well, what the hell. Life is life, I guess.

How is it going? It is going very well thank you. Life is a real peach. I now have a ring and chain that are both 24 karat. Together they are worth about $1,000. This week I bought a beautiful jade ring and huge jade Buddha with a $300 chain. I think I will send the 24-karat stuff home. My son, Mark may want the stuff after I am dead. We never know when dead will happen.

Linh has proposed a banking business arrangement to me that is similar to a "loan shark" in the USA. I will give it some consideration. She needs something to do besides taking care of the house.

The way the business works is that she lends my money at a very high interest rate to Vietnamese who need money and spends most of her time riding around on a Honda collecting the daily interest on the loans. Several Vietnamese have created their own banking system rather than trust the government with the little cash they save. It seems women all over the world are tired of taking care of home and family. Linh and I had a short discussion on the value of staying home just the other day.

I completed my eighth Vietnamese language lesson this morning. I enjoy studying the language. My teacher is a gay guy, that works at a nearby hotel. It seems like there are a lot of gay people in Vietnam.

That is it for now. I still have another two hours to wait for the plane to arrive. Patience is a virtue in Vietnam.

Thursday, March 11, 1998

I just finished another meeting with the Under Secretary of Ministry of Posts and Telecommunications here in Cambodia. I am getting cleaned up, and then it's off to a full night of dinners and maybe later a little drinking. Okay, so I had one beer already this afternoon. The guys are picking me up in one hour to go to dinner.

Besides that what is going on? Oh, I stayed in the hotel last night. That is a first for me. I was tired, so I went to bed early and slept until about 7:30 am this morning with only minor awakenings during the night.

Life is a real twist, isn't it? What the hell are you doing in Vietnam? Oh, by the way, Russell's so-called wife is pregnant with Tam's so-called baby. Isn't that the way it goes for us GIs?

Not much else to write about except that sales suck because of the currency crisis and overall economic slowdown. Business-wise, things are not going well. I have to get some business going, or I will be looking for work next February when my contract is up. I burned my leg on the Honda while Dai and I were in Vung Tau. It is still bothering me some. Life is what it is, right? I sure like the ring I had made from my one-ounce panda gold piece. It is a fine piece of jewelry.

Friday, March 20, 1998

Made it back from Cambodia and only had one bad night while I was there if you know what I mean. On Monday of this week, I go to Hanoi for three days. Last weekend Linh was still in Can Tho, and I drank too much again. I got so drunk my bladder let go and I pissed my pants. A very good man brought me home and stayed with me until I was sober enough to go to bed. He kept me away from the women too. I have not had a beer since. I am trying to cut back or quit. I may have trouble with the Hanoi government if I do not take it easy. They do not like Americans up there much anyway, let alone drunk ones.

Linh's son moved back in with us today, and I bought a new Honda motorcycle yesterday for $1,650. I need my own transportation while I am here and Linh will end up with it when I leave Vietnam or die.

That's about it for now.

Saturday, March 21, 1998

His name is Phuc Le. He is Dai's father. He was young once and strong. He is a tall man for being Vietnamese. That is perhaps why he was selected to assist the American Special Forces during the war.

He was shot twice and lost many friends during the war and then was left behind when the Americans decided to go home. He spent the next many years in re-education camps. After completing his time there, he worked as a cyclo driver (a bicycle three-wheel carriage) until the booze and smoke took his health. When I met him, he was coughing up blood and didn't have the money for food or medicine. He is out of the hospital now and is still very frail and weak. He weighed maybe a hundred pounds and spent two weeks in bed at the hospital with a bag dripping in his arm.

In the morning he and I will go to the Buddhist temple and thank the gods for allowing him to live a while longer. Most people in this country die from lack of money. Perhaps, he will be one that lives a while longer.

Wednesday, March 25, 1998

Isn't that interesting? I was drunk again last night here in Hanoi and slept with another prostitute. Well, I didn't exactly sleep; I got to sleep about 5:00 am and had an appointment at 9:00 am. I was only a few minutes late being the good drunk that I am. Then I went out and had a couple of beers at lunch with Ross.

How many women has it been in the past nine months? I know it has been many. I will be lucky if I don't get AIDS or something like it. I am not too proud of myself. I am starting to feel an obligation to the woman I am living with again.

I have another meeting with customers in the morning then back to HCMC in the afternoon. That is about it for now.

Tuesday, March 31, 1998

It has been a while since I wrote. Life is still about the same. I got drunk on Sunday and went to work on Monday. Linh's son, My Lai, has moved in with us. It is good to add a little stability into the structure; if you know what I mean? Of course, you don't. You are not a real person. You are just a piece of paper letting me write this stuff on you.

Let's see what else. Oh, I finally got a hold of the retirement group. I should be getting a check sometime next month. I am only getting a total of about $1,400 after taxes and Donna' fifty percent. Life sucks then we spend money. I now have over $20k in my checking account with close to a $100k in my 401k. Add my $24k for the land value and life is a beach?

I will say goodbye for now because I just ran out of medications (That is my antidepressants) and Copenhagen. It should be a fun time in the next few days.

Friday, April 17, 1998

Today is Mary's sixteenth birthday. I will call her in the morning. It will be the 17th there then.

I need to write about my last drunk. It was a bad one. I went drinking with Dai my security guy. Somewhere around 10:00 pm, I lost contact with reality in a major blackout. Some person tried to take my wallet on Hai Ba Trung Street. Apparently, I broke his nose and knocked him out. When he woke up, I continued to fight with him and his friends. My right hand was all swollen up the next day. I had a bruise on my cheekbone and blood all over my shirt.

I very easily could have killed him, or his six friends could have killed me. Dai said he knew most of the other guys and was able to keep them off me. I banged around a lot that night. Linh finally found me in a bar on Pham Nu Lao Street. I even fought with her trying to get me home. Later I vomited all over the bed and myself. A really pretty picture I'm sure. I talked to Donna and asked her for a phone number of AA here in HCMC. She gave me a number, but it isn't any good.

Short memory, last night the American Chamber of Commerce had a new guy party. I had two glasses of wine and came home. I think king alcohol has scared the crap out of me for a while anyway. I may have the bad guys (Vietnamese mafia) looking for me now.

Linh and I were on the outs for several days. She said that if it happens again, she will leave. That is probably a good idea for her and her son. However, without her support, I would have been dead by now. Not much else to write. It is another slow day at work.

I can't seem to get anything going on the job. Only have a couple of weeks left before the big conference here with my boss and sales team.

Saturday, April 18, 1998

Called Mary this morning but she had left with a friend. I guess they are having the party in the morning. Not much going on here. I have been staying close to the house since last Sunday's bad day. (It was a really bad day!)

The rains started last night, and it has been raining off and on all day. The monsoons will last about six months. That should be a joy. Linh and I had another big argument last night. It seems we keep running into issues concerning money. Actually, the money is going very well. Rent is only $200 a month, and Linh does all of the cleaning, cooking and food purchasing for about $200 a week. Not bad, I guess. I am saving about $6,000 a month. I think. I am just about done with a book called *Chickenhawk*. It is about Vietnam of course. And I am still taking Vietnamese language training every morning with my private teacher.

I have only written ten pages this year. That is not much considering what has been going on. Goodbye for now.

Sunday, April 26, 1998

Today is my happy birthday. I am fifty-one years old. Fifty-two in Vietnam as is the custom. Here they assume you are a year old when you are born. It makes sense when you think about it.

Yes, I drank beer this past weekend. Friday night went out with

Miss Phuc and Miss Linh, shot some pool and drank beer; later Miss Linh was very sick and throwing up everything, and I left to drink some more. I got home about 3:00 am. Something like that.

My job gets more difficult every day. My boss is very upset about the lack of sales in Vietnam. Richard's contract has ended now. Next week he will find out if he has a new contract or not. Who knows maybe the company will pull out of Vietnam altogether.

Week after next is the staff meeting. I have very little good news to report. In fact, I have no good news to report. The senior manager will be here checking me out. Oh well. It doesn't mean anything to me anyway. That is about it for now. My back is a little sore today. Been having too much sex I guess.

Strange life it is, I don't know where it will all end. I hope it will end in Minnesota or Vegas. At least I feel that way today. Don't know about much going forward.

Tuesday, May 4, 1998

Good morning Vietnam from the top floor of the Equatorial Hotel in beautiful downtown HCMC at 6:00 am in the morning. We are having our midyear staff meeting here in this crappy town. I had dinner with about twenty-three people last night. Yesterday I spoke to my boss about my presentation. He had me reduce it by fifty percent. He said to keep it short and sweet. I guess he likes the new and fresh type of report.

I had another bad blow out last Thursday and Friday. It was a big holiday here for the twenty-third anniversary of the fall of Saigon. I celebrated with another one of my familiar drunken, pants pissing, blackouts. I took the cleaning lady (twenty-five years old) on a bus trip to Vung Tau while Linh was in Can Tho. We came back Saturday morning to face a waiting Linh. She was livid. She was dressed and waiting for a Honda to take her to Vung Tau to retrieve us. The good news is I did not sleep with the young girl.

Linh left again yesterday to go back to Can Tho and buy a house. The cost to me was around $5,800. The communist government rewards former Vietcong who had a difficult time during the war with a small house. The least we Americans can do is reward a child that we left behind with one small house. (It is actually a very large house on the Mekong River in Can Tho.) Who knows, it could change her entire life. I like the idea of a lost street girl becoming a homeowner.

I don't know how long I will be here, but now I believe I will be back even if the contract finishes next February. The house will provide me with a place to stay whenever I am here. Truth is if I could get off the booze, I could have a decent life here with Miss Linh. She is perhaps the strongest willed person I have ever met. She is as tough as the roughest kid on the streets of Saigon, and inside, she is fearless, and I believe she can commit to someone long term. But I may not be ready yet for any firm commitment.

Monday, May 11, 1998

Well, last week is over. The staff meeting went very well. I have no sales, but I think I made a lot of brownie points with the management. I am still drinking too much though. I was drunk again last night and two nights last week. A friend and I made the rounds a couple of times last week.

There isn't much else going on. I just got an e-mail from one of my old customers in the US. A few other people that I worked with have sent their regards, but outside of that, it is the same old stuff. Oh, I bought a house for Linh. I guess you already knew that. I know I have a place to live here the rest of my life if I want. My boss told me I do not have to worry about job security. I guess that is encouraging.

Tuesday, May 19, 1998

I spent last weekend in Can Tho with Linh. We went swimming in the Mekong River a few times and spent some time seeing her new house and meeting some people. We spent a lot of time with her second family. (The Vietcong family that took her in as a young slave girl.) Her dad is in charge of his district for the Peoples Party Committee.

Linh will be moving into the house soon. She is leaving in two weeks. I told her last night it is the right thing for her to do. She must go live with her son in the Delta. I will live here alone.

I am so sad. The nightmares have started again. Vietcong are trying to kill me in my sleep. Rashes are coming back on my arms. Still, have them on my right leg. I am taking pills for depression. Doctor Nancy is sending VA medications all the way to Vietnam.

I sent a nasty letter to Susan about letting my brother live on my land. Enough said.

Sunday, May 24, 1998

Another day is about done in the land with no sun. Linh is moving out next Friday. She will be moving to her new house. I will be alone for the first time since I got to Vietnam. In some ways, I am looking forward to it. In others, I am a little concerned. Last Friday I had another bad drunk and another, pants pissing, blackout. Guess I came home and raised hell here. I placed a knife to my throat and threatened to kill myself in front of Linh. It will be the same old story. Just one more dead Vietnam Vet and no one will give a damn.

Anyway, I suggested that it might be best if she moved to Can Tho. I may go and visit later. The booze is getting bad. I drank about eight big BGI's then I don't remember anything else until about 4:30 am in the morning when I was lost and wandering the streets of Saigon alone. One more month and I go home to see the kids. I am looking forward to that. I hope I make it that long.

I have to go to Danang and Cambodia before I leave and one more trip to Hanoi too. That should keep me busy for the next month; I hope.

Friday, May 29, 1998

Yesterday Linh left for Can Tho and took everything with her. I guess I did not think about her taking all the furniture and kitchen stuff. I have a bed, a plastic lawn chair, a coffee table, and that is about it. My rashes are acting up again. They are on my butt, arms, and legs. It must be my nerves or something. I spent last night in the house alone. It has been one week today since my last drink. I don't know if I can make it sober tonight though.

I am becoming very distressed with the people here. Everyone is after money. They don't give a damn about anything but your money. Matter of fact, I am feeling like crap. I only had one bowl of soup yesterday. I am down to a hundred and seventy pounds. I must force myself to eat another bowl of soup today. I have had no hunger feelings for the past couple of weeks.

The job is pretty screwed up too. It seems like they are paying me to sit on my butt. I am waiting for my distributor to produce something, and nothing is coming through them.

I might stay sober tonight just to spite the rest of the world. The people here want me drunk, so they can take my money. That is except Linh; I still can't figure her out. Either she is smarter than the rest, or she really cares about what happens to me.

Damn rashes again! Itch like hell whenever I stop to think for a minute. Last night was rough. I kept waking up with sweats and dreams. Drinking and killing dreams mostly. What else. Guess that is about it for now.

Damn, I need a drink!

Saturday, May 30, 1998

Well, I didn't make it through the night sober. Met Dai about 9:00 pm last night and drank all night. I got home sometime this morning. At least I did not have a blackout, and I only spent about sixty dollars. I do not know where that much money went in one night of drinking, but it did.

Donna called this morning, and we had a long conversation. She said she still loves me and always will. She wants me to stay at the house with her when I return to the states. I told her that I have been living with Linh for quite some time and that she left a couple of days ago.

I am confused. What do I do with the rest of my life? Stay here or move back to the states? I must admit I am getting a little tired of this country and its greedy people. The problem is the job and Linh. I miss her a lot. I have gotten myself into quite a mess.

Now I have one foot in Nam and one in America and pissing on everything between.

My stomach is messed up today, so I only slept a couple of hours this afternoon. Life is a bit of a beach. At least it is nice to be wanted in two different worlds. I guess. Maybe the truth is that I am not wanted in either and don't fit in either.

MARTHA'S ACCIDENT

June 9, 1998

I got a call here in Hanoi that my daughter Martha had a car accident and is in intensive care in Las Vegas. I need to get a ticket out of here and see if she is going to be all right. She rolled a car five times with her daughter Sofia in the back seat strapped into a car seat. I called my boss and told him that I was going home and would use my vacation. He said that would be fine since I have two weeks' vacation coming anyway.

Sunday, June 28, 1998

I have been back in Vietnam a couple of days. Martha had a car accident and was in intensive care for about a week. She is fine now. I spent a week on the land with Sonny and spent some time with my sister Jenny. It was okay, but I was in a hurry to get back to my Miss Linh. Now Linh and I are talking about marriage.

Where are we going? Linh met me the night before I went to the United States and met me the day I got back. I don't know if it is the money or the honey for sure, but she is very good for me;

this I know for sure. Where do we go from here? Martha and Sofia are fine. So I guess we will survive another day or two. Today I had about four liters of beer and felt a little tipsy, but Linh came and brought me home. As I said, she is good for me. Wife, this I don't know if I am ready for it. In fact, I am not ready for it.

We drink, drink and die, or we live, live and die. It is all the same anyway. Enjoy it while you have it and never forget our anthem -- Screw it; it don't mean nothing!

Love ya too much!

Wednesday, July 1, 1998

I had another bad drinking night last night. I got into a fight at the Apocalypse bar. I hit some big Australian guy. He said something to me about how I was addressing a lady friend of his. I must have hit him pretty hard because the knuckles on my right hand are all swollen up and sore today.

I don't know what it will take to get off the booze, but I need to find out. Linh and I have been talking about getting marriage papers. She told me yesterday that she did not want to do that. Too difficult she said.

My thinking has been crazy. One day I am going to stay in Vietnam forever, and the next I am ready to go home. My thinking has been very crazy. That is for sure. I am certain it is the booze. I am going to Cambodia next week. It is not easy to stay off the booze there. The 4th of July is this Saturday, and it is not easy to stay off the booze then either.

But whatever I do, I MUST quit drinking soon or end up dead, or in jail for the rest of my life.

Sunday, July 5, 1998

Linh left a couple of hours ago. We had a very nice week together, minus the one night of course. I still do not trust her or anyone else. It costs me a couple of hundred a week to keep her around, and she is well worth it; I might add. I just do not know where it is all going. Now she tells me that she will not marry me. Her reasons are quite modest. She does not want to jeopardize my relationship with my kids; both financially and emotionally. She also thinks I need to go home to get off the alcohol.

We have been talking about getting the papers since I got back from the USA, but she tells me that we can live together and do what we want without the legal papers. The only conflict is when we stay at hotels we must rent separate rooms.

I believe Linh has saved my life several times since I got over here. She is one special kind of person. She takes good care of me, her son, herself, the house, my money, and everything else with which she comes in contact. Her only problem with me is the drinking. By the way, I was sober four days this week.

Yesterday I went to a customer meeting with my distributor and had a couple of beers. Once it got in my blood, I immediately wanted to go downtown. I tried to create a problem with Linh that would allow me to do just that but it didn't work. She forced me into talking about some stuff and in no time, at all I was out of my bag and stayed home to a peaceful evening. I thanked her for being my head doctor for the night.

In the morning, I go to Cambodia. I am nervous about this trip. The conditions are not good there right now with the elections and all. They have had over one hundred and seventy incidents of violence in the past month with four people killed in the streets.

There are too many guns in that country. They may even have more than America.

There is not much else going on except the Vietnamese government wants me to pay about $14,000 in back taxes. I appealed it and should hear something this week. If they take too much; I may just quit the job and go home, or quit and stay here, or quit and move to Can Tho, or quit. The chances are good that I will not quit. I need to keep this job because it gives me purpose. Without it and Linh, I doubt that I would be around; if you know what I mean? Sometime I will write and tell you about Linh. She has an amazing life story. She was homeless most of her life without family or friends. She now has a house and hope for a good future.

Dai was over today. He sold his cyclo, and his child is in the hospital. He needed money real bad. I was ready to give him a hundred dollars when I got the look from Linh. We ended up giving him about $25. That will get him some medicine for the kid and a little food. He had not eaten in a couple of days. Life is a joke for some people I guess. It sucks for the poor and homeless in Vietnam.

THIRD TRIP TO CAMBODIA

Wednesday, July 22, 1998

It always seems to happen in July. Linh went home last Thursday, and I have been raising hell ever since. I called her yesterday early morning. I felt really bad. I had been drinking most of the night. I ranted at her and told her to just stay in Can Tho because I didn't need her anyway.

I called her again this afternoon. She was in a very upbeat mood. She said, "Now I ask you one question." "Do you love me? If you do, we get married." I was surprised that she asked since we have been talking about "just living together." Anyway, she went to Long Xuyen yesterday afternoon. It is a five-hour Honda ride from her house. She checked with the local government in Long Xuyen about marrying a foreigner. She has all the information.

My answer to her question was yes, I do love her. Now, do I really love her? Who knows for sure? I know I do not want to live alone. I know I have no desire to live with Donna again. But I am scared about the prospect of marrying Linh. The problem is that I am having a tough time living my own life right now. So here is a little excursion:

Reasons why it is a good idea:

1. Linh is a good lady that cares about me.
2. We can live anywhere without legal problems.
3. My emotional, sexual, and other needs will be well taken care of by her.
4. She is a great cook. It is fun to travel with her. I like our house in Can Tho.
5. She might give me a reason to live again.

Reasons why it may not be a good idea:

1. My drinking problem.
2. Legal and financial considerations.
3. My kids would not approve.
4. Her son is a handful, and I don't deal well with little kids.
5. We would have to live apart a lot of the time.
6. So, the only advantage is a legal living situation in Vietnam.

I don't know. It feels scary. I know that I miss her when she is gone. I hate my life without her. When she is not here, my life consists of booze, prostitutes, and casinos. I don't think either Linh or I have the capacity to feel this thing called love, but we do need each other for our own selfish reasons. Mine are mostly emotional, hers perhaps financial security and her son. I believe that is the truth of it. The other truth is I do not want to be alone. And, I do not want just any good looking body. There are plenty of them around. I want someone that needs me. Pretty basic stuff, I guess. I told her I would come down to Can Tho tomorrow and we can talk further. She said to be sure to bring my birth certificate and divorce papers. We will see where it all goes.

Wednesday, July 29, 1998

I had a great weekend down in Can Tho. Linh and I went on a couple of long Honda rides. We took one bike ride to Long Xuyen to check on getting marriage papers. The second trip was across the river to the Buddhist Temple at Chau Doc to query Buddha and the other gods on what we should do. We decided to get married, but when we got back here on Monday, I got cold feet. It is a big decision for me. I like the idea of being a free man. I like to come and go as I please. I know, however, that every day I spend with her brings me closer to "getting the papers" as she calls it. She is one heck of a lady. She has been alone her whole life with nobody to care for her.

I know she will be here for me as long as I want her to be, with or without the stupid papers. Our love life is good, and we spend hours just talking alone in our empty house. We have time. This I believe.

That is it for now.

TRIP TO LAOS

Thursday, August 6, 1998

It is another night in wonderful downtown HCMC. I got back from my first trip to Laos yesterday. Linh has been down in the Mekong Delta at the house for the past week. She is coming back on Saturday morning, early. Things in Laos were very quiet. I visited several Buddhist Temples in Vientiane. There were some very old and beautiful ones. I also visited their propaganda war museum. They had a ton of pictures of our CIA war in Laos back in the 60's. I found it to be interesting, but very slanted.

I had a couple of bad drinking days while I was there. The first day of drinking, I made the irrational decision to take a boat up the Mekong River into the jungles of Laos and not come back. I bought the ticket for a riverboat and planned to leave the next day. The plan was to go up the river to end it all.

That night I was sitting in a bar about two in the morning. I was the only person in the bar except for the bartender who was serving me booze. I was shocked to see a young Caucasian woman walk in the door and call out, "Does anyone in here speak English?" I said, "I do. What do you want?" She came over and told me that she was backpacking through Laos and that a bus had just dropped her off. She said she had looked around and there were no hotels open and she needed a place to stay for the night. I told her I had a room down the street with two beds and she was welcome to have one of them, but I was not done drinking. I invited her to come over, sit down, and have a drink.

She came over and ordered a coke. I asked her if she was sure she didn't want something a little stronger like snake whiskey. She said, "No thanks, I don't drink. I am in AA. I have two years of sobriety." She said she was a Peace Corp worker from America and that she had been working in Kurdistan for nearly a year.

Sometime later that night I ended up passed out in my room. When I woke up, I found a handwritten note on a piece of cheap toilet paper from the Peace Corps worker. She wrote:

"To the honorable one. God works in mysterious ways. See you in an AA meeting next year." It was signed T.M.

She also left me a brass temple lion as a gift. I sat there on the bed and began to cry. How could someone from AA find this lonely drunk here in one of the darkest corners of the world? God had sent me an angel to give me hope. I got up, walked down to the river, and canceled my ticket to nowhere.

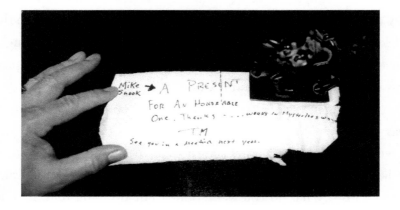

Back to HCMC:

Since I gave Linh the earrings, I feel more committed to the relationship, but I hate giving her money. It just does not feel right even when she doesn't ask for it. Susan is planning on coming to Vietnam in November for a couple of weeks. That should be interesting having her here. Also, next week is Ross's last week with the company. It is going to be a tough week for him. Chuck is coming from Singapore and wants me to escort him to the Hanoi office and take care of his affairs. I feel bad for Ross; his boss didn't do right by him that is for sure.

Sunday, August 16, 1998

Today is the first day of the rest of our lives. How are you doing Mr. Journal? I am doing just peachy. I have been drinking for the last two days straight. I stayed up all night, and this morning, about five woke up Mr. Dai had him rent a bike and take me to the Pagoda in Na Bear to burn some incense to the gods. I got back home around noon.

Called Miss Linh and asked her to hurry back to HCMC. I don't like to sleep alone. Good title for a song. Huh? Anyway, she has a small business going in Can Tho now. She is selling duck soup and making quite a hit at it, I might add. The soup sells out in about two hours every morning. It sounds like she is having a good time with it too. She said everyone asks her why she has to sell soup when she has a rich husband. She tells them that she likes selling soup, so I guess it is up to her.

I went to our Hanoi office last Friday with Chuck from Singapore. He was here to kiss Ross goodbye. It was a sad week for Ross. He is no longer employed. He is an older guy that has been around

Vietnam since the 1960's. He has a Vietnamese wife and loves it here. I don't know what he will do now. People in Vietnam tend to lose their foreign spouse when the money runs out.

For the time being, I am the only company country manager left in Vietnam with four Vietnamese reporting to me. I don't know where that is all going. I may end up the only one, or they may add a person later. But for now, some guy in Malaysia is going to be covering Ross's job from Thailand. That should be interesting. Huh? Sorry, it sounds like I am talking to myself because I guess I am. I hate being alone in the house. Guess I will check my lottery tickets see if I won anything. However, there is a slim chance of that.

Saturday, August 22, 1998

What a week it has been. It has been another really bad week. Last night I lost my wallet with $400 in it. I also lost my credit cards. That is not good. I started drinking around one o'clock in the afternoon. I drank a quart of wild turkey then went drinking with Cary, a one-handed Canadian guy that lives near me. He thinks I lost the wallet in a taxi. But the chances are good that someone took the thing out of my pocket at the bar.

Linh's grandmother died last Tuesday night. I went down to Can Tho Wednesday and came back early Friday morning. The funeral was quite an event. Cost us about seven hundred dollars with more than one hundred people eating for three days. I think I met damn near every person in Can Tho.

I am a real pain in the ass; possessive and self-centered to the extreme. Linh had to stay an additional three days because three days after her grandmother is put in the ground the family must go back and carry a dead chicken around the gravesite so that she will realize she is dead and can go to the moon.

I called Linh last night in a major huff and cussed her out in Vietnamese for not coming home with me and causing me to lose my wallet.

I spoke to her today and said I was sorry. She sure has put up with a lot of stuff from me. Hard to believe she is doing it for the money. Must be that she really does care about me. I know everyone in Vietnam believes we are already married and refers to me as Linh's husband.

I have been doing well about staying away from other women. That is not sleeping with anyone else now for quite a while. I guess since I gave Linh the earrings. Anyway, I know that the only way I will be able to finish this contract is if Linh is here with me. Alone I will die from the booze. I have been drinking for weeks on a daily basis. I cannot even get drunk or sober any longer. Last night I tried to pick a fight with five men in a soup place. I yelled a bunch of curses at them. I am lucky to be alive.

BRISBANE AUSTRALIA TRIP

Friday, September 4, 1998

I am on the plane flying from Australia to Singapore. I have been in Brisbane since last Tuesday. I met with Anita and her husband Larry. He is a former Marine lieutenant and thinks he may want to go back and visit Vietnam. However, he does not seem like he is quite ready for such a venture yet. He had a tough time over in Nam. Trained the Kit Carson scouts. (Chieu Hoi folks.) He speaks good Vietnamese but still has a lot of conflict going on. He is retired, wealthy, and somewhat bored. He wants to visit for a few days. I may invite him to come for a visit later.

I spent a week with the North Asia team. Had a good time but I am worn out. I will meet with Darryl and Mitch this afternoon and return to Vietnam in the morning. It is a long flight, seven hours. I went to the casino in Australia, had a pretty good time, and met some very interesting people. There were mostly Chinese and Japanese people at the casinos. It was quite an honor that I was the only guy invited from the South Asia team to meet with Anita's husband, Larry.

Things are changing within the management group. I believe we will be moving under Mitch shortly. That could be good or bad depending on what they want to do in Vietnam. I did some drinking but never got drunk while I was there.

Anyway, there isn't much else going on. I left last Sunday and felt tired. I found out about my boss's management style. That is enough said about that. Actually, he is a bit of an arrogant jerk.

Monday, September 7, 1998

What a weekend and day today. I drank all weekend, went in this morning, and quit my job. I called my boss and told him to terminate my contract; I am going home. Rumor on the street is that Linh is back with her husband. I do not know how long that has been going on; however, I believe it is true.

I will be returning to the US in a couple of weeks. I must get some help with the drinking. I had a long talk with Donna about it the other day. There isn't much else to say. I am feeling really messed up lately. Booze. I can't even get drunk anymore, just keep drinking all day and all night. I feel bad about a lot of things. I know I need help or I will die here.

THE END OF THE ROAD

The end of all things is near. Be alert and of sober mind.

1Peter 4:7 (TLB)

It was my last trip out of HCMC before returning to the United States. I had survived my trip to Vientiane Laos. Linh had left me alone at the house. She was gone and had taken everything when she left. I had just quit my contract. The darkness surrounded me.

The monsoons were horrific. It was raining sheets night and day. We had not seen the sun in over a month. I was drinking whiskey every day. I was no longer able to get drunk or get sober. I was near the end of the road.

Sometime during the night, I woke Dai from his sleep. He was sleeping in his cyclo again with a poncho wrapped around him. I was drenched in the rain and sweating from the humidity and heat. I shook Dai awake and told him I needed to go to Vung Tau.

Dai was the only thread left between hell and me. He had been committed by his father to keep me alive as long as I was in the country. His dad was a former special forces ARVN that served with the Americans during the war. I saved his fathers life soon after coming back to Vietnam in 1997. He had been vomiting blood for about a week, and I spent some money to get him into a hospital. He was suffering from esophageal hemorrhaging from years of drinking rotgut beer and rice whiskey. After a couple of weeks in the hospital, he got out, looked me up and gave me his son for security for as long as I was in Vietnam.

So Dai was all that was left at that point in my drinking. He agreed to rent a small Honda bike and take me to Vung Tau. I don't know how long it took us to get there in the rain. I don't know how long we stayed after we arrived. Time frames are lost in the dark fog of alcoholism.

I remember only glimpses of time during our stay. There was bar drinking the first few days then it was drinking alone at the place we were renting. Dai would never drink. His sole purpose was to keep me alive. I was an insane, ranting drunk that had extreme outbursts of rage at people and objects around me.

We had this game that I would play. When Dai would fall asleep, I would disappear, and he would have to find me. I would grab a taxi and have the driver take me to the darkest parts of town that he could find.

One of these dark nights I was stumbling around downtown Vung Tau looking for a barber that would shave my head. In Vietnam, there are only three types of people that shave their heads. The first are Buddhist Monks. The second are people who have lost someone and are in deep grief. The third type are people who no longer have a reason to live and are ready to die. I was in the last group.

I was stumbling around in the dark pounding on doors trying to find someone who would shave my head. Somehow, due to the chaos that I created, Dai was able to find me. He tried to talk me into going back to the room, but I would have nothing to do with it. I was going to get my head shaved that night.

We woke up two barbers that refused to shave my head because they knew they would be complicit in my death. We finally found a man that was willing to risk his own trip to hell by cutting my hair. He was hesitant but shaved it all off.

A few days later, I was in our room hung over. It was late afternoon based on the Seiko on my wrist. I had just come to and dunked my upper body in the cement rain cistern in the middle of our room. We may have been there a week maybe two, but this was the first time that the drunken stupor had lifted sufficiently for me to see myself in the dirty mirror. I was not a pretty sight. I was no longer an American. I was Vietnamese. I looked like Dai's drunken father. My face was shrunk and hollow looking. I was wearing only a pair of red boxer shorts and sandals. What I saw in the mirror was a standing ravaged dead monk. I weighed about 160 pounds. My teeth had a yellow scum covering them, and I was bald. I submerged my upper body in the cold water one more time and went to wake up Dai. It was time to go home.

I remember looking in my wallet to see if I had any money left. My money was gone, but I still had a credit card. I had a moment of clarity and realized that I could get a ticket with the card and maybe go home to America. It was merely a choice of doing that or cutting my wrists and slowly bleeding out.

It was a long, dark, and wet ride back to HCMC. We were both wearing green military ponchos but were completely soaked to the bone. We had to stop many times because Dai couldn't see the road. We stopped at one place and had coffee. I decided I needed to buy the orange robe of a Buddhist Monk. The people at the coffee place knew of a place down the road that sold robes, and I ended up buying one.

I bought a ticket home the same day we got back! We waited outside the ticket office for several hours for it to open. I got the ticket for a departure in a couple of weeks. I needed some time to tie up some loose ends. Dai helped me find a room to rent for a couple of weeks. I needed to get the stuff out of my house and shut it down before I could leave.

Things were really bad. I was sick and could not keep food down. I spent the next couple of weeks alone in the nasty little room. Dai would come and visit every other day and bring me food to attempt to eat. I was at the point where I had to drink something during the day, or the shakes would be so bad I could not get out of bed.

I was not able to return to my house because the Vietnamese mafia was looking for me. There was nowhere left in Vietnam that was safe. I had to get out of the country or be killed. Dai would come, pick me up at night with his cyclo, and take me to different places to close down my living arrangements. I did not want to see any of the people that lived near my house. I do not know what they thought. I think they believed that I was dead somewhere.

Toward the end of the two weeks, I had Dai take me to the house and load up the remaining clothes, a few pieces of cookware, lawn chair and coffee table. It was very late at night. I know it was after midnight. As I was leaving, walking behind Dai and the cyclo, I notice a boy standing against a wall watching us. I don't know how long he had been standing there, but somehow he knew that I was leaving.

I recognized the boy. It was the young gay boy who hung around the neighborhood. It was the same boy that several months earlier I had saved from a group of kids that were beating him in front of one of the bars on Pham Nu Lao Street. I guess he had remembered and had been watching for me to come back to move. It was not uncommon to see kids standing around wanting a foreigner to give them a handout, but this was very late at night.

I dug through the junk in the cyclo and found a little white teddy bear that I had bought Linh for her birthday. I walked over and handed it to the boy. I will always be able to see that boy standing in the dark shadows clinging to the little white teddy bear. The rest of the stuff ended up with Dai and his small family. The next morning I was on a plane back to Las Vegas.

VA PSYCHIATRIC WARD CONFINEMENT #3

I was drunk when I got to Las Vegas. Somehow, I made it back to the house in Summerlin and spent the night. The next morning I woke up early and went down to the garage where we had set up a couple of couches and chairs. Donna would usually have her coffee and cigarettes in the garage lounge area before she went to work. We were talking about how things had been going with the kids. I was hung over and was not able to concentrate very well.

She told me that she had made a list of all of her bills on a yellow legal tablet and handed it to me to read, Meanwhile, she got up to get some more coffee. I do not know why but I thumbed through the tablet and came across a letter that she had written to her married boyfriend. After quickly reading it, I sat there in stunned silence. The stark reality of what had been taking place during the last two years finally hit me like a ton of bricks.

When Donna walked back into the garage a few minutes later, I stood up and walked out. I knew at that point that our relationship was over. The trust had been so violated that it would never return for me. I got dressed and left the house.

Later that morning I found my way to the AA Kiss (keep it simple stupid) Club. They had a 10:00 am meeting that I attended. My head was still swirling from the alcohol and the shock of the letter. I was telling the group that I was desperate for sobriety. I said that I had been sober for eighteen years and I knew what I needed to do to get sober again. I told them that I knew I needed to find an AA sponsor, read the Big Book, get on my knees in the morning, ask God to help get me sober, work the twelve steps, and go to AA meetings.

I was still rambling on when this short little old lady stood up down at the end of the table and yelled, "You need to shut up! You don't have a clue about what you need to do to get sober again. You are not an old timer in AA, you are a newcomer, and you better start acting like one."

I sat there with my mouth dropped open as she continued, "And I'll tell you something else about yourself. You are the type of crazy bastard that is going to get a gun, go downtown, get up on one of those tall buildings and start shooting people. So you need to get your butt up and immediately check into the VA psych ward.

I got up from my chair and walked out the door. Boston Joey, as she was called, saved my life and perhaps the lives of many other people that day. She could not possibly have known that I had thought about that very thing numerous times when I was downtown in the crowds. She could not possibly have known that I had two AK-47's and hundreds of rounds of 7.62 mm ammo in my storage shed.

I left the club and caught a cab to the VA. I think this trip to the Las Vegas VA psych ward meant that I was finally ready to get help. I remember nothing about my time there. I must have been detoxing from the alcohol most of the time. I have no idea how long I was in the hospital, but I know that the day I got out, I caught the next flight to Kansas City.

RETURN TO KANSAS CITY

The trip back to Kansas City was one of defeat. I was going backward, but I knew that if I had any chance of getting sober, it would be in Kansas City. I would have to go back to the AA club where I had been sober before and face the people with whom I had worked during my time at their club. I hoped that the people I had sponsored when I had eighteen years sobriety would now be able to tell me how to get sober again.

Northeast Johnson County (NEJC) is an AA club for a wide range of alcoholics. We have everything from doctors and lawyers to drug addicts and homeless. It is located in downtown Overland Park, Kansas. We like to refer to our club as the "last house on the block." For many of us, that is exactly what it is. We have nowhere else to go. If we can't get sober at NEJC, we will end up "locked up or covered up."

When I got back to NEJC, I knew that I was one of those people that had nowhere else to go. I had nowhere to live. I had just gotten out of my third trip to the psych ward. I was about as lost and alone as I had ever been in my life. In addition to that, I was a raging alcoholic that was not willing to listen to anyone. I had made a conscious decision never to trust another human being as long as I lived. I was convinced that I would never get close to anyone ever again.

My memory is not that great, but I remember moving into a

Motel 8 a few miles from the AA club. I might have been there a couple of weeks. I still had some cash in the bank, so I rented a car to get around. A few weeks after getting to Kansas City, I moved into an apartment. It was a small two-bedroom unit. I moved into the smaller bedroom and threw a blanket on the floor until I could buy a sleeping bag.

I decided that I would decorate my new place with all Asian stuff, so I found a place not too far from me to start buying furniture from Asia. The place was called F.O.B., and an American ran it with his Korean wife. Most of the stuff they had was from Southeast Asia. That was what I was looking for, so I started buying Buddha statues and bamboo furniture. I bought an antique Chinese opium bed and set it up in the large bedroom. I placed a four-foot statue of Buddha on the wood bed and two large Buddhas on either side and began to spend time meditating on my cushion and burning incense to the gods of Asia. I also went back to the Vietnamese Buddhist Temple over on White Street in Kansas City, Missouri.

I completed my apartment décor with a bamboo love seat and coffee table and a couple of very large Asian screens. I spent several thousand dollars before I was done fixing up the apartment. I also bought an expensive rice cooker and numerous cans of sardines for food. I was not able to adjust to American food at that point.

Sometime during that first six months, I decided to go back to Vietnam and be a Buddhist monk. I spoke with the monk at the Vietnamese temple in Kansas City and asked him to contact the Dalat Buddhist Temple in Vietnam and see if they would accept me as a novice monk. He contacted them, and they agreed that I could come and live in a beautiful temple up in the mountains of central Vietnam. I was ready to go. I only had to order my visa. I filled out the paperwork and started the process of returning to Vietnam.

A few days later, in a telephone conversation, I mentioned my plans to my AA sponsor Corky H. He told me to stay home because he was on his way over. When Corky got to the apartment, he told me to get on the phone, call the local monk, and tell him to contact the temple in Vietnam because I was not leaving Kansas City. He sat there and waited for me to call and tell the monk. I really didn't have much choice. It is a good thing because I would have been drunk as soon as I hit Saigon. I would never have made it to any Buddhist temple.

Realizing how close I came to leaving the country; I decided it was time for me to check into the Veterans Administration in Kansas. I saw a psychiatrist who filled the numerous drug orders that I had received at the Las Vegas VA psych ward. I also started to see June a therapist at the PTSD clinic located at the VA. I saw her weekly for the next year. (I think she retired from the VA after her last session with me.)

I was unable to work for that first year back because the anti-psychotic drugs heavily sedated me. Sometime during the first six months, I bought a small house three blocks from the AA club and started going to meetings every day and hanging out at the club when I was not in a meeting. I moved all of my Asian furniture to the house and continued to buy statues to fill it. After moving, I drove back to Vegas to get my things out of storage which was mainly guns and ammo. I did all of these routine activities, but I was not getting any more normal. I was still very sick, and the craving for alcohol was with me constantly during that first year back.

Then I met a girl at the AA club. She was beautiful, intelligent, blond, and she had a great body. Her name was Lori, and eventually, she became my wife. She would wear these really short cut-off blue jeans, and I would follow them around everywhere they would go. We had a rather stormy romance in the beginning, mainly because I was still so sick and unable to get close to anyone. The first conversation Lori and I ever had was about trust and how neither of us would ever be able to trust another human being. She had been divorced for the same reason that I had. I continued to have some contact with my ex-wife and Linh while I was pursuing Lori at the club. That first year was not a smooth transition. I spent most afternoons napping from the medications and then had trouble sleeping at night because of nightmares. The following two entries were the only two recorded after returning to Kansas City.

Tuesday, November 03, 1998

It is another day in Kansas City. I just got back to the apartment from an AA meeting at NEJC. I went to eat with some guys. I was very tired earlier. I have been thinking about Linh a lot since I spoke to her. I am not sure that I want to be sucked into sending more money to her. That money thing has always been a problem for me. Not much else to say. I will be adding some writings on paper that I did in the VA hospital. I just got back online this afternoon. I spent about five hours updating this stupid computer.

Thursday, November 5, 1998

It has been a couple of tough days. I have been talking to Linh again. I sent her four hundred dollars to help out, and as soon as the money was wired, I started feeling used and distrustful. She said her sister had been hit by a car and Linh had to borrow a couple of hundred to help the family. I do not believe it, and I told her so. Why can't I just let it go?

I spent several hours at the VA yesterday checking in. I am

starting to have panic attacks again, and I have begun taking the VA medications. They have me on an antipsychotic drug. Oh well, I guess that is the way life goes.

Also, Linh said she would "show me around Vietnam" when I come back to visit. I do not need a guide. I need someone like her with whom I can spend the rest of my life. She still refused to come to the USA.

And that is how it is.

III
FROM DARKNESS TO GRACE

". .the darkness is passing away, and the true light is already shining."

—1 John 2:8

A New Beginning

The first year back in Kansas City was difficult. Near the end of 1999, I reduced my anti-psychotic medication to where I was able to function better in society. Before lowering the drug dosage, I was having difficulty with my memory. I would be driving and get lost in my neighborhood. The drug was very good at blocking intrusive memories of Vietnam but had significant side effects. I was sleeping for several hours every afternoon too.

I tried to work sometime during the middle of 1999, but that only lasted a couple of days. One of my old working buddies started their own distribution business and needed a partner/sales manager. I was doing fine until he told me that he expected me to work out of his basement. The desk was too small, and the expectation that I was to be at work every day was too daunting. I told him that I changed my mind; however, the truth was that I was not yet ready to go back to work.

Another friend of mine contacted me in early January 2000 and told me about a job opportunity with another communications company. It was in their distribution division as a product manager. I was told it could lead to a sales job in the future. I went in for the interview and got the job. Working again was a major adjustment. I had to show up for work and spend the whole day in a cubical for the first time in several years.

June 2000 was a turning point for my sobriety and my life. I mentioned earlier that the craving for alcohol had been with me since getting sober at the end of 1998. The overwhelming desire resulted in a relapse back into active alcoholism. Looking back on it now, I know that the obsession probably never left because I was taking such a heavy dosage of the antipsychotic drug from the VA.

The relapse occurred while I was on a business trip. I was attending a big telecommunication event in Atlanta. A business acquaintance and I were in a bar having a sandwich, and he was drinking a dark beer. As we got up to leave, he said, "Maybe after we get checked into the hotel we should get together and have a few drinks."

We were walking out the door, but I turned to him, and replied, "That sounds like a great idea, but before we leave I need to try one of those fancy dark beers that you just had." That response was the beginning of a weeklong drunk after more than a year of somewhat good sobriety. Most of my drinking was done alone that week because I am not very social when I drink. My hotel had a bar downstairs, and my rental car could get me to the nearest liquor store. I was set for a good drunk.

I got back to Kansas City on Friday that week and was drinking on the plane on the return trip. I remember stocking the trunk of my car with booze and going to the VFW, which I thought, was a "safe" place for me to drink. I closed the VFW down and went to a bar in downtown Overland Park. I think it closed at two or three in the morning. At least I had the good sense to park my car at my house and walk to that last bar. It was only a few blocks from the house.

I left the bar when it closed at 3:00 am and fell in the street out behind the NEJC AA club. A man came, picked me up, and carried me to my house. I think it was the guy that lived across the street from me, but I am not sure. The person sat on the couch with me for a while then disappeared.

The next morning I called Corky, and we met at the club to have what is known in AA as a first-step meeting. Tom, one of the guys that I used to sponsor, was in the meeting. I turned to Corky and in a shaky voice said, "I don't know if I will be able to get sober again." I felt hopeless.

Tom yelled from the end of the table, "Well, damn it Michael none of us can get sober again without help. That's what the hell we are doing here!" He got up and walked out of the meeting. I am not sure what happened then but something changed inside of me.

I went back to my house after the meeting, sat down with all my Buddha statues and took a good look at myself. I was a hopeless drunk. I was beyond human help. I knew at that point that if I could not find God, I would die a drunk. I noticed a Bible was sitting on my dining room table. I remembered having picked it up in my hotel room in Atlanta before I checked out. I opened it and tried to read some verses, but the words had no meaning.

I began to cry. I picked up the phone and called Pastor Teasley. He had been my pastor when I was a child in northern Minnesota. I thank God that he answered the phone that day. I told him the whole story. I told him about the PTSD, the divorce, the relapse, the return to Vietnam, the psych wards, and now another drunken relapse. I told him that I was a hopelessly lost sinner that had become a Buddhist idol worshipper and I needed God's help.

Reverend Teasley asked me to get on my knees, and he said the Jesus prayer with me. I gave my life to Christ during that prayer. It was June 11, 2000; Reverend Teasley told me to read the Bible and pray daily. I got up off the floor a redeemed person.

I placed the hotel Bible on the dining room table and began reading it on page one. It took a year to read the Bible, and I didn't understand much of the Old Testament, but I read it anyway. The miracle of God's grace is that the craving for alcohol was removed while I was on my knees that day and has not returned.

In July of 2000, despite the alcoholic relapse, I was promoted to regional sales manager for my company's wireless markets. Having to go to work every day had been stressful enough, but now I would be on the sales roller coaster. I assembled a team of sales reps from my old friends at my former company and went to work.

The money began to roll in, and my relationship with Lori was getting better by the day. She had gotten sober in January 2000 after a relapse, so we were both busy with going to AA meetings, working, and staying sober. We had taken a vacation to Florida in early spring 2001, and I proposed to her shortly after getting back home. We bought a house in Leawood, Kansas and married in October of 2001.

We took a trip to beautiful Hawaii for our honeymoon and had a wonderful week on the beach. However, during the week in Hawaii, I had a call from my company and was told that they had a significant layoff, which would affect my sales team and me. I finally talked my way into getting a two-level downgrade rather than lose my job, but my team was not so fortunate. They all lost their jobs while Lori and I were on our honeymoon.

The next two years I was gone most of the time on business trips. I had sales responsibility for Minnesota. I would leave Monday morning and get back to Kansas City on Thursday night. I became acquainted with my new wife and stepson on the phone and on the weekends.

The stress level was high in my new job. In December of 2003, I received a verbal warning because my Minnesota sales numbers were under objective for the year. The next month they rewarded my slow sales year by adding another state to my territory. They added North Dakota in the middle of winter. Now I was expected to leave on Sunday or Monday and travel both frigid states all week.

After being on the road for four weeks straight, I finally was burned out from the pressure. I was working a trade show in Fargo, North Dakota. I set up the booth managed it and tried to entertain customers at night. I was ready for a nervous breakdown. I left the show early, went home and told Lori that I did not think I could go back on the road the following Monday. She suggested that I call the company employee resources people. I spoke with a counselor, and she placed me on short-term disability the same day. Later she wrote a letter that was helpful in getting my disability with Social Security. I had worked in telecommunications for thirty-seven years, and that was enough. I was burned out and no longer able to work.

During the rest of 2003, I completed the company's long-term disability benefits program and applied for un-employability at the VA. My therapist at the Vet Center sent a letter to the VA as well. I later applied for and was awarded, Social Security Disability as well.

Now that I was no longer working, I spent every day at NEJC AA attending meetings.

THE GOD JOURNAL

I have waited for your salvation, O Lord!

Genesis 49:18

The second journal is merely called "The God Journal." It is a continuation of the path from darkness toward God's grace. Lori and I attended the Billy Graham crusade when it was here in Kansas City on October 10, 2004. We both felt compelled to go forward at the altar call and recommit our lives to the Lord. We were already born again believers before our recommitment, but it was a good feeling to make a statement for Christ publicly.

Shortly after we were at the crusade, we decided that we needed to find a church home. So, we started visiting different churches in our area. We checked out the mega-churches and the small neighborhood churches. We had a church near us that sent someone to our house after the Billy Graham event. They gave us a follow-up basket of things that included a cup. The church was Emmanuel Baptist Church (EBC). We continued to try other churches but finally ended up at EBC in December 2005.

The people were wonderful to us. They helped us to become involved in an adult Sunday School class and a Life Group. Lori and I both joined the church through baptism by immersion. The pastor was a brilliant man and was an outstanding preacher. We enjoyed our time and activities with the church. For the first time in years, we felt like we were being fed the word of God.

In June of that year, we were asked by the church if we would be willing to start a Celebrate Recovery type program. We visited a few of the Celebrate Recovery groups around Kansas City and finally decided that we would start our program based upon the twelve steps of Alcoholics Anonymous. We called it Soul-Care Recovery.

The following is a two-year journal of events that took place during our stay at EBC.

Saturday, January 1, 2006

When we walk through the storm, we cannot see the stars. Nevertheless, when the rain stops you can see all the way to the moon.

- Old man sitting near the alley entrance, tattered knee-length coat for warmth.
- Been six days no food – soup line closed – no more soup.
- Seems like long time not happy, only sit alone with his shadow.
- The smell of sandalwood scent seeps under the door.
- The thought returns – can't go home no more.
- Why on God's green earth would the lady,
- Sit on the ground next to the naked dead baby?

Monday, February 6, 2006

Dear Lord,

This weekend Lori & I will be baptized at Emmanuel Baptist Church. We will be "dipped" to represent your death, burial and resurrection. Lord, I seek forgiveness for the many sins I have committed against you.

Father, forgive me for I have been a thief by not returning the many material gifts that you have given me. "Thou shall have no other God's before me!" This is my biggest sin Lord – please forgive me and give me a clean heart so that I may better serve you, Lord I am unworthy of your grace or forgiveness – please Lord allow me mercy for these trespasses.

Help me, Father, to know you better!

Monday, February 27, 2006

The Lord, The Lord, the compassionate and gracious God, slow to anger, abounding in love and faithfulness.

—Exodus 34:6 (NIV)

Father your mercy is beyond my ability to comprehend. You have delivered me from the miry pit and placed my feet on solid ground. I thank you, Lord, for your unending mercy.

Father, I hunger for your word to be placed in my heart. You have removed my "heart of stone" and given me a "heart of flesh" a tender heart that is receptive to being filled by thy Word and Spirit. Thank you, Father.

After two days of fasting, you gave me a vision of John and me in church where you led him to the altar to accept Christ as his

Savior. I thank you Lord for speaking to me through the Holy Spirit and allowing me to see the future event happening. The vision was on February 24, 2006, and I shared it with John yesterday.

Lord your grace is sufficient for my needs. Lead me to a closer love relationship with you Father.

Thursday, March 2, 2006

Lord, I thank you for your mercy and grace. Your word is a lamp unto my feet and a light unto my path. Thank you, Father.

Today Lord I must learn to separate my Christian fellowship from my AA fellowship. According to my lovely wife, I have occasionally been preaching in meetings. I should only lead those who are being led by God. For it is God's work, not mine. I am a lost sinner that is an empty vessel being molded by God, perhaps to be of use to him someday in some way. Lord Have Mercy!

Father, if it is thy will, help me to be closer to you today than yesterday. Allow me to be a living sacrifice for you. Only by my weak example can I show God's changing work in my life. Lori said we demonstrate God's work by being examples.

I love you, Father Jesus! Please allow me love, peace and hope this day Lord. Your grace is sufficient for all my needs.

Thank you, Jesus!

Tuesday, March 14, 2006

Let us approach God's throne of grace with confidence, so that we may receive mercy and find grace to help us in our time of need.

—Hebrews 4:16 (NIV)

Lord, allow me to boldly go before your throne of grace and obtain your mercy and receive your grace for all my needs. Lord your grace is sufficient for my needs.

There is calmness in the air today. The sun shines in all its glory. "If we live in the Spirit, let us also walk in the Spirit."

Yesterday I walked another five miles. Lord help me remember that my relationship with you is all that is important in my life. Today help me to pray unceasingly, constantly, always, everywhere, all the time.

Yesterday you placed Larry behind me to answer a question. Today he is helping remodel our bathroom. All things happen for the glory of the Lord. Amen.

I must always remember this. It is what happened to me.

> ²⁴*For I will take you from among the heathen, and gather you out of all countries, and will bring you into your own land.*
> ²⁵ *Then will I sprinkle clean water upon you, and ye shall be clean: from all your filthiness, and from all your idols, will I cleanse you.*
> ²⁶ *A new heart also will I give you, and a new spirit will I put within you: and I will take away the stony heart out of your flesh, and I will give you a heart of flesh.*

²⁷ And I will put my spirit within you, and cause you to walk in my statutes, and ye shall keep my judgments, and do them.
²⁸ And ye shall dwell in the land that I gave to your fathers, and ye shall be my people, and I will be your God.

—Ezekiel 36: 24-28

Monday, April 17, 2006

Saturday we went downtown to "feed the people." What a wonderful thing to do. It was very moving. Easter we went to adult Sunday school. After church, we had Sara, Martha and Lori's family and grandkids over for an egg hunt.

These are glorious days to be with the Lord! Jesus did reveal himself to me during Sunday school and again later in the sanctuary. I clearly saw a vision of him. He was very tall and transparent. Praise God for his grace and mercy!

Thursday, August 17, 2006

It is God who works in you to will and to act according to his good purpose.

—Phil. 2:13 (NIV)

I am back to reading God's word in our Jesus room. My communication has not been good for some time now. I believe my actions have "Quenched the Spirit." I still struggle with my gambling issue. The Lord keeps letting me know that it is a sin against him. Lord help me to repent of this sin and turn back to you today.

Soul-care group has been going on for a couple of months, but our numbers are dropping. Lori and I pray every morning for God's guidance in our lives.

I recall the story about the man that wanted to follow Jesus but when Jesus said, "Sell everything and follow me." he turned and walked away because he was a very rich man. I believe it was in Billy Graham's devotional today. Lord help me not to be like that man. Help me never to turn and walk away from the Lord again. I praise you, Father. Amen.

Tuesday, September 12, 2006

Heavenly Father, I thank you for your grace and mercy. Thank you for another day of sobriety.

Let your light so shine before men, that they may see your good works, and glorify your Father who is in heaven. Matt. 5:16 (KJV)

Lord help me to complete the awesome task that you have asked of me. The road is often not clear, and there are many stumbling blocks along the way. Some days you seem far away, and the communication is not there.

Sometimes, Lord, my light seems like a fading candle. However, I do know this: your grace is always there for me. Thank you, Father, for your Mercy. It allows me to live this day in peace.

In Jesus name. Amen.

Friday, September 15, 2006

Satan is attacking me at every turn. A few weeks ago, he caused me to fall and hit my head in the kitchen, and I spent the night in the hospital. Doctors still do not know what caused it to happen.

Yesterday, I was sitting on the toilet when people cleaning the sewer lines caused the water to back up and get feces all over the seat, the carpet, and me. It was just like something out of the movie *The Exorcist*. I was sitting there reading Billy Graham's devotional book. Lord have mercy on me!

These things are occurring on Thursday. The day our Soul-Care group meets. For some reason, Satan does not want me to have the recovery group at the church. But I will not turn back from my walk with Christ. I will not be deterred. It only encourages me to complete the task set before me. The task is to become more like Christ. Amen

Friday, September 22, 2006

Today is the first day of the rest of my life, and I am grateful to God for it. My heart is heavy this week because my son Mark has a very serious gambling problem. He called last Friday and said he had blown his whole paycheck check at the casino. He was afraid to go home and tell Jackie.

His mom and boss (Charlie) were going to meet with him yesterday evening to talk about what he is going to do to get help. Charlie is in AA and is willing to go to gambling anonymous (GA) meetings with Mark to help him. Mark also has gotten caught up in the payday loan garbage and is way over his head in debt. He wanted me to bail him out, and I had to tell him no. I love him too much to pay his gambling debts. But I pray for him every day. Lord have mercy on my Son!

Lori and I spend a lot of money at the casino here in town. I do not feel okay with that anymore. I have been asking the Lord to give me the strength to let go of my gambling compulsion. We are covering all our bills and saving money and giving money to the church but I still don't feel good about flushing money down the casino toilet. Now with Mark having a serious problem with gambling, it is pushing me to give it up as well. Lord have mercy on my son and me.

Tuesday, September 26, 2006

It is another day in the life of Michael. I feel like we are turning a corner in the gambling thing. Lori and I went last Friday night and lost another $500 after the grandkids were here. I have been praying for God to help me ever since. Pastor Larry preached on the rich man story and said we are all holding one thing behind our back in our fist and God wants it. Mine is gambling, and I am now ready to give it to the Lord.

Pastor Larry said we also have something in our pocket and the Lord will want that after we give him what is behind our back. The Father wants all of us. And I am willing to give it all to him today.

I have been nominated to the ministry counsel as a member at large. I guess that is quite an honor. We meet once a month to talk about the church business. Should be rewarding but it is also another motivator for me to be a better example of a "born again believer."

Yesterday I was praying in our Jesus room and had a strange reaction to the scripture that I was reading. Shaking and groaning came out of me. It felt like something was removed from the inside of me, something evil and dark. Been feeling better ever since. Went to south lake park and saw homeless Bill. Spent some time talking to him about the grace of God and what it has done in my life. Praise the Lord! It is going to be another wonderful day walking in the Spirit.

Being born again in the Spirit is the next gift that the Lord wants for me. It will happen if I continue to let go of the things that block me from the communications with the person of the Spirit, which resides within me. Praise the Lord! It is a glorious day to be alive through the grace of God!

Monday, October 02, 2006

Today Martha and I will go to the neurologist to find out what they are going to do about her brain tumor. She found out last Thursday that she had one. She woke up in the morning with Bell's palsy, had a cat scan and found the tumor. The tumor is not connected to the Bell's palsy, or so the doctor said on Friday.

This is the third major event that has happened on Thursday. Soul Care group meets on Thursday. Several people think Satan is trying to derail our program. However, I don't want to give any power to the devil that he doesn't deserve.

Not much else to write about. I am angry at Mark and Martha's inability to manage their money.

Thursday, October 05, 2006

Praise the Lord! The brain tumor is not going to be any problem according to the surgeon. That is wonderful news for Martha and the family. Tonight is Soul Care group. We are supposed to have some new people from AA attending. That should be exciting. Love you, Father!

Friday, October 27, 2006

Yesterday during a meeting at NEJC, I openly confessed Jesus Christ as my one and only Higher Power. I also told the group about Soul-Care Recovery group. We have been leading the program for four months now. It was a pretty scary thing to do with my AA friends. The topic was on our spirituality. So, Lord use me at the AA club in any way that you see fit. We are stepping out for Christ in a powerful way and need your guidance, Lord.

Fill me, Father with the indwelling Spirit.

Saturday, November 03, 2006

A few days ago, I destroyed a hard copy of my 1993-1999 journals. I burned it in a fire in the grill out back. I also destroyed all soft copies of the journal. If God can forgive and forget my past, who am I to hang on to it? Thank you, Lord Jesus! I feel lighter and brighter today more than I have for a while.

We had a great Soul Care group meeting again last night. Eight people were there sharing themselves with each other. The group has exceeded my expectations for reaching the needy. We have several people that are "beyond human help." I would definitely include myself in that harsh group.

Praise the Lord for He is good!

Thursday, November 09, 2006

Lord, these last few days have been busy. People coming to do the tile in the bathroom, and Jeb is here getting ready to do the sheet-rock in the basement, and waiting to hear from the guys with the epoxy, and the leaves everywhere on the ground and I reached 187 pounds yesterday, the lowest I have been in a year, and tonight we have the recovery group, and the Republicans lost the election in both the house and the Senate. Lord have mercy. Let it slow down so that I may take more time to spend in my relationship with you. The one-hour walks, the time in our Jesus room, the one-hour naps. Lord let me slowdown that I may spend more time with you.

I thank you, Father, for all the blessings that you have given me. Thank you Lord for your grace and mercy and bringing me back from the darkness of alcohol addiction to this wonderful new life. Your blessings are too many to count.

Thank you, Father!

Thursday, November 30, 2006

I have been sick for the last week with the twenty-four-hour flu and sinus infection. I finally went to the VA and got some antibiotics to start getting better. Corky and I have been clashing some the last few weeks. We had a bit of a go around the day before yesterday. He thinks I am very sick and that I have been that way for several months. He suggested that I take an inventory.

Mary should have my tenth grandchild this morning. She has been in the hospital a couple of days waiting on the baby. Hope to hear something early this morning. The baby's name will be Grace. I will always know her as "Grace" because it is only through God's loving grace that she will be born sometime this morning and after she is born, I will be praising the Lord the rest of the day. Thank you, Father.

If the truth were known, it is only through God's loving mercy that I have been here since 1998 to see, most of my grandchildren born. We do not ask for justice; we pray for His mercy.

Thank you, Father.

Tuesday, January 2, 2007

Well, it is a new year. What a wonderous-glory-filled year 2006 was. It may have been the best year of my life. So many spiritual things happened. EBC has been a blessing. Soul-Care Recovery has been a blessing. The Lord has been a blessing.

On New Year's Eve day, I was called by God to perform a baptism of one of our group members at EBC. What a wonderful event it was. Rita fell down the stairs in front of her apartment on the way to church, but she called and told me that Satan was not going to stop her from being baptized that morning. She was very determined. The Lord is good.

Praise you, Father!

Wednesday, January 3, 2007

God has directed me to give up gambling. We have wasted too much money over the past five years. Last Friday, December 29, 2006, we had a miserable time at the casino spending $500. I pray that it will be my last time.

The Lord has been giving me this command for a long time,

but I have refused to comply. Last Friday he made it very clear that if I want to follow Him, I must comply with this command.

He sent a Seraphim with a hot coal to burn my lips. It removed my inequities and cleansed me from my sin. Praise the Lord! Isaiah 6: 7 was revealed to me by the Lord. I received a burned lower lip and saw the angel at Harrah's casino. Praise the Lord! I wanted to make sure that He would give me the strength to do this thing. I believe that Ed was sent to the restaurant at the casino last Friday to give me a sign from God that I needed to quit. Help me, Father! Give me the strength that I need!

Praise you, Father!

Monday, January 15, 2007

Urgings from the person of the Holy Spirit:

Jun. 11, 2000	I surrendered my life to Christ. Quit drinking alcohol. Began reading the Bible – completed in one year. Began giving away the Buddhist idols.
Oct. 04, 2004	Billy Graham revival. We recommitted our lives to Christ.
Dec. 06, 2005	Joined Emmanuel Baptist Church.
Feb. 13, 2006	Baptized at EBC by immersion.
Jun. 11, 2006	Started Soul-Care Recovery at EBC.
Jan. 01, 2007	Began Tithing at church.

The list is so brief and incomplete. The Lord has been good to us these past several years. We praise you, Father!

Thursday, February 15, 2007

In the next day or so, we will have our Soul-Care web page activated on the church website. What a wonderful tool for us to glorify the Lord. It is very exciting. Lori and I have added our stories. It is scary to be that transparent in front of our church, but it is important if we are to reach the people in need.

The Lord is good today!

Thursday, March 1, 2007

It has been a while since I wrote. We just got back from Vegas and California. We were out there for six nights. We enjoyed the time with Lori's sister, and we spent time with the kids. I saw our new grandbaby.

Yesterday Soul-Care went on the internet. It is scary having our personal stories online, but we hope it will help someone find the road to recovery. I have wanted to do some writing but cannot get myself to sit down and type. I found a soft copy, on a backup disc, of my old journal. I have been working on that some.

I started gambling again last month. I made it a month and a half without it. I feel somewhat separate from God right now, but I do not think anything can separate me from the love of God. I just need to spend more time in the word and on my knees.

Jimmy is going home from the hospital in Saint Louis tomorrow. Thank you Jesus.

Praise God!

Monday, March 19, 2007

Yesterday a friend of mine came over to the house and told us that he was unsure of his salvation. He said he had never said the sinner's prayer with another person. He asked if I would take him through the act of salvation. We did so up in our Jesus room. Praise the Lord for He is good!

We also had our life group over to the house last night. They were here for three hours. We watched the end of the KU basketball game. They just won their second game in the NCAA tournament. We get so much out of our life group. We have a new couple, Pat and Linda. They are very well versed in the Bible. Pat has been a pastor at a couple of places before.

Lord, help me to be the person that you would have me be but help me also not to change so much that I am beyond the people you want me to reach. The Apostle Paul said, "I became weak that I might gain the weak."

Thursday, April 5, 2007

My son Mark is going through a very rough time right now. He has lost about everything because of his gambling addiction. He has been living at his mom's home for three weeks. He has lost his apartment, his wife, and his truck has been repossessed by the bank. He is a mess.

He called me a week ago and told me that Jackie had an affair with some other guy. He is completely torn up about it. He wanted to know if he could borrow $18k from me. I told him no that he would have to let the truck be sold at auction and get a cheaper one.

I spoke to him last night for about an hour. He is buying a $600 truck today. He is consumed with the breakup of his relationship. He is angry, confused, lonely and lost. The good news is he has not gambled now in three weeks. He has been seeing Jackie and the kids, and they are still talking. She is not yet able to let go of the other guy. Mark is reliving my divorce ordeal exactly ten years later. Lord have mercy. He is in the same house, the same month; his wife has left him for another man, he is confused, angry, blaming himself, in denial about what is going on, and overall a real mess. His mother has left him alone in that house for a couple of weeks while she is in Minnesota helping her mom. Thank God, that he has several good friends and he's been taking care of his daughters at night. However, it has got to be a real nightmare for him because he was in that evil house in March 1997 after Donna left.

I am not sure what the message is for me from the Lord in all of this, but I can only encourage Mark to get professional help. He is not feeling well physically either. He said he has bad circulation and needs to see a doctor about a lump on his chest.

Please be with my son Father. I trust that you know what is best for him. I place my son into your loving arms Lord. Draw him to you Father

Monday, April 9, 2007

Yesterday I spoke at two church services. I gave a brief testimony about my alcoholism. I just got a call from a lady who has an alcoholic husband who is in real bad shape with his drinking. Praise the Lord! It made my statement in front of the church worthwhile. Thank you, God.

My son called today too. He is about to give up on his marriage. He is thinking about divorce. Be with him, Father.

Tuesday, April 10, 2007

We heard from Rita today. She and Jeff are back together after a relapse and want to come back to the AA group. I believe that if God can bring me home from Vietnam, He can bring Rita and Jeff from their relapse into a life of recovery under grace. The love I have for AA is immense. In today's meeting, we talked about taking our eye off the ball. God saved my soul, but AA saved my ass.

Praise the Lord and thank you, Father, for accepting me just as I am; a simple-minded sinner like me. In 1998, there was no hope for me, and yet today God has graced me with a wonderfully blessed life. I am so grateful that it brings tears to my eyes when I think about it.

Thursday, April 26, 2007

Praise the Lord this sinner has made it to sixty years old! What a wonderful life it has been these past seven years. I feel so blessed by our Creator. "What a friend we have in Jesus."

Today I will receive two gifts, a Bible of my choosing and a gun. I have decided to buy a CZ 75 P01 9mm pistol so that I can carry it with my concealed carry weapons license.

The Bible is not so easy. I struggled with the gun too. I am not sure how much I need it but oh well. Kids will be kids.

I have looked at dozens of Bibles trying to get the right one. So here is what I am looking for:

1. A word for word translation not a thought for thought.
2. That means an NKJV Bible
3. Maybe large print
4. Genuine leather
5. Red letter
6. Wide margin
7. Ministers Bible - maybe
8. Cambridge or Oxford

Something very strange happened to me this morning. I was pouring my second cup of coffee, and I had a visual experience of me in the house in Vegas ten years ago this morning. I know exactly what I was doing because of my journal entry that morning about 2:00 am.

I was completely alone in that house with my guns. I was a few weeks away from drinking, a few months away from divorce, a few weeks away from returning to Vietnam, a few months away from early retirement and I was very suicidal.

I saw this vision and started crying. However, they were tears of gratitude to the Lord for his grace in bringing me to sixty years of age. I turned fifty in that room, and today I turned sixty with a wonderfully blessed life. I was unable to stop the tears. I went into the living room, got down on my knees, and started thanking Jesus.

I was still crying, so I went upstairs and spoke with Lori who was in the bathroom. She wanted to know what happened to me. I said I didn't know, but I couldn't stop crying. She held me and let me cry on her shoulder. What a tender moment. Thank you, Jesus.

It was a wonderful spiritual experience. I was letting go of something. I praise the Lord every day for allowing me to see another day of His unmerited grace.

Thank you, Jesus.

Monday, May 7, 2007

Last week was a special week of helping at the church, in Soul-Care and helping people in AA. I have a new sponsee. His name is Larry.

I stopped gambling again. The Holy Spirit is really working on me about this area of my life. Lori and I went the night of April 28th. We had a birthday party for me and went to the boats. I hit a fifteen hundred dollar jackpot. I don't feel good about winning, and I don't like wasting money. Nevertheless, the most important thing is the constant urging of the Spirit to let it go. Sin breaks the communication with the Lord. I would rather hear the words of Jesus than any other thing. I want to tear down all things that get in the way of my Lord and me.

I want to hear the voice of Jesus and see Him again. Thank you, Father.

Wednesday, June 13, 2007

So much has happened that I cannot write it all down. Rita died, and we had a funeral. I have a sobriety birthday this week. Soul-Care is one year old this week. Praise the Lord. We are getting the house painted. We had water in the basement and had to tear out the carpet. We installed a $2,100 sump pump to prevent the water from coming back.

Lord, there is so much going on. The kids are okay. Sara is

getting another house in which to live. Martha is moving into an apartment. Mark lost his wife and got her back, lost his job and got it back. Mary thinks Bob is having a nervous breakdown because of something occurring at his previous company.

Lori and I are doing fantastic. Most days are full of peace and plenty. We praise the Lord every day for his love and mercy.

Thursday, July 12, 2007

Father, I am so weak in the flesh. I know that I do not confess you before all men because of my fragile ego. Help me to be stronger in my faith. Fill me, Lord, with joy that others might worship and praise you more. Father, I still struggle with the casinos. I have learned that as a weak human being I still love my children when they stray. However, I am disappointed when they struggle. Lord, I am sure that many times you are frustrated with me. Father, I need your reassurance that you love me even when I am weak.

Help me, Father, to understand your word better. I have been reading Watchman Nee books the past few months. I have just realized there is only one interpretation that matters and that is the interpretation of the Holy Spirit.

Father, help me to slow down my mind throughout the day to talk to you. Help me to be still and listen for the voice of the Spirit.

Father, July is always a difficult time for me. I humbly ask for your help in getting me through another July with a calm mind and a pure heart.

Father thanks for giving me a heart of flesh. I praise you for your grace and your mercy Lord.

Thursday, July 19, 2007

The death of my father and my sister happened on this date. My return from Vietnam in 1969 happened today.

- Thank you, Lord, for protecting my family and me this day.
- Thank you, Lord, for being with Jenny during her surgery this morning.
- Thank you, Lord, for keeping me sane and safe this day.
- Thank you, Lord, for your many rich blessings in my life today.
- Thank you, Lord, for your gift of sobriety and sanity for me.
- Thank you, Lord, for the magnificent life you have given me.
- Thank you, Lord, for your grace.
- Thank you, Lord, for your mercy.
- Thank you Jesus!

Wednesday, August 1, 2007

Praise you, Jesus! It is another blessed month with the Lord. We sold our car yesterday and bought a jeep. Wow! It is really a thrill to drive it. Thank you Jesus!

Sara came over last night. Cody and I fixed the light on her car then we went for a walk with Neal and her. I love that boy. What a privilege it is to be able to spend time with my children and grandchildren. Thank you, Jesus.

We are still working on the basement. Richard is doing an

excellent job on the remodel. Praise Jesus! He is a good Christian man.

This is a copy of an old gratitude list:

I am grateful to God's grace for the following:

- Sobriety
- AA
- Return to Sanity
- Physical well-being
- Mental well-being
- Spiritual well-being
- Removal of the cravings for alcohol
- Return to my wonderful country
- Freedom not to have to work

I am grateful for the people He has placed in my life:

- Lori
- Cody
- Sara
- Martha
- Mark
- Mary
- Sonny
- All ten wonderful grandkids

I am grateful for my AA Friends:

- Bob T.
- Corky and Linda
- Don S.

- Tim H.
- Boston Joey
- Mike S.
- Ron
- Hank
- Hugh
- Jim L.

I am especially grateful for the people who have influenced my life the most:

- Pastor Teasley
- Jerry and Maryann
- Corky
- Mom
- Dr. Nancy

I am grateful for the material stuff:

- Wonderful clean air
- America
- Birds
- Green grass
- Our home
- Air conditioning
- Shoes
- Enough money to live on
- Walks with Lori and Cody
- One hour naps in the Asian room

My new life goals:

- Serve my Lord and Savior Jesus Christ.
- Continue to develop a strong personal relationship with the Lord.
- Spend time with my kids and grandkids.
- Serve my fellow man.
- Live in the present as much as possible.
- Serve others with my truck.

Tuesday, August 28, 2007

It is another wonderful day of living in God's grace. We finally finished the basement work. It looks great. Just in time for watching some football games. Praise the Lord.

I am waiting to hear from Richard to see if he will come back and add the last piece to finish the project. The handrail going downstairs will be the last item to be installed. We are also waiting on delivery of a new loveseat for the upstairs family room. The Lord is so good to me today. Seven years of sobriety by His grace and mercy.

Thank you, Jesus!

Wednesday, October 3, 2007

We just got back from Vegas visiting the kids. I continue to gamble and feel bad. Lord Jesus, help me to give it up and trust you.

We did have a wonderful time with the kids on this trip. We went to a carnival, soccer game, Chucky Cheese and just spent a lot of time with Mark and Mary and their kids.

Dennis wanted me to co-teach a Sunday school class with him

starting this Sunday. After talking with Lori and Corky, and many prayers, I had to tell him thanks but declined. I never know what is best for me even when it comes to serving the Lord.

But I know this: I desire to do the Lords will. I also know that I am here only due to God's grace and unending love toward me.

Thank you Jesus!

Wednesday, October 31, 2007

Another day in the life of a Christian soldier. NEJC is planning to close the doors over the next couple of months. That may not be such a big deal except that I have been going there for over twenty years, and I have depended on the help of the people there to keep me clean and sober for most of that period of time. I was drunk for a couple of years 1997 and 1998.

Anyway, I have started looking around at some church meetings to see if I can find a place where I am comfortable going to meetings. I guess there is not much else happening. We will be feeding the Halloween monsters tonight. Sara will be bringing the kids over later for trick or treats.

Wednesday, November 14, 2007

Yesterday I had a flashback at the PTSD meeting. I had to leave the session. Bob and Dave went outside with me and after it was over Dave and I rode around in his truck for an hour before I went back to meet with Ronda. It is scary to know I can have those attacks even when I am on my medication. A woman named Bev brought up a man that she had been talking to at the 25th Vietnam Memorial Day celebration in DC last weekend.

The man's name was Russell. I knew him in Vietnam in 1997 and 1998. It just really freaked me out. I got home and took a two-hour walk in the trails to try to shake it off.

I am feeling better today. Hope I can go on from this thing. Russell and I have a dark history in Ho Chi Minh City.

Friday, November 23, 2007

Yesterday was Thanksgiving. We had Sara, Mary, and their kids over along with Jackie, Susan and Jackie's kids. Sonny, Betsy, and Lee are coming down today to spend a couple of nights. That should be interesting. I am looking forward to seeing them.

I wonder where it is all going. I am trying to stay away from the casinos again. With the Lord's help, I might make it this time. The Lord gave me a word. He said that not only are we stewards of all the material and relational gifts he has let us use while we are here, but we are stewards of His grace as well. Having His grace carries a specific responsibility. Think of that: material stuff will come and go but the Lord's grace cannot be denied nor diminished. It is so evident in my personal story. Thank you Jesus!

> *Then Jesus spoke again to them, saying, "I am the light of the world: he that followeth me shall not walk in darkness, but shall have the light of life."*

> —John 8:12

Thank you, Jesus, for your light and life!

Saturday, December 1, 2007

Who among us can ever live in complete obedience to the Word? Surely not me. I continue to fail in my pursuit of holiness. However, I continue to ask the Lord for mercy and grace.

In the last couple of days, I have shifted my way of thinking about Christianity. I cannot be the person that I think God wants me to be and I continue to fail in my attempts. I know that this is exactly why Jesus had to die on the cross for me.

Now I have caused stress in my marriage because of my continued self-loathing regarding gambling and my inflexible approach to religion. Recently I was asked to teach an adult Sunday school class. My ego jumped at the idea even though I am chairing Soul-Care. Lori thought I might be taking on too much and I finally agreed with her and turned down the offer. I am having a lot of trouble separating God's grace from the legalistic demands of the Old Testament. Lord, have mercy.

I am so obsessed with my walk with the Lord that, at times, I cannot see the path on which I am walking. Lord, have mercy on me, a sinner.

Wednesday, December 5, 2007

Can a man descend so far into the darkness that he cannot be saved by the light of Christ? Satan has been working on me this last couple of weeks. He would like me to turn from the path that the Lord has laid out for me. I will not turn! Lord, I plead the blood of Christ that was shed on the cross, that while I was yet a sinner, He died for me. Thank you, Jesus.

Lord I love you with all that I am. Holy is the Lamb! I am

listening to a great band called Desert Reign. Lori and I saw them at Homers coffee shop.

Lord, sometimes I am so sad about the lives of the people near me. Our children continue to struggle. Lord, have mercy and lay your grace on them.

Mark continues to struggle with his marital issues and gambling. Now he has joined a biker gang and nearly was killed in a motorcycle accident a couple of weeks ago. Lord Jesus, have mercy and grace on my son and draw him to you.

Mary is getting married this month to a man she has known for over ten years. She is working as a craps dealer in a casino in Las Vegas. Her road has not been easy. Lord, have mercy on Mary and bless her and Bob this month as they commit to their marriage.

Martha continues to struggle with health issues. She is a single mom that is devoted to her daughter Sofia. She has an inner-strength that carries her through, but, Lord, I know that personal strength is not sufficient. Lord, shed your mercy and grace upon Martha and Sofia. Help them, Father, to know you.

Thursday, January 10, 2008

"Then Jesus was led by the Spirit into the wilderness to be tempted by Satan."

—Matthew 4:1

"Thus you are to know in your heart that the LORD your God was disciplining you just as a man disciplines his son.

—Deuteronomy 8:5

What would you say or do to your son if he was pulling away from you? Would you love him more or less? Would you love him no matter what he does, or how far he strays from your expectations of him?

I love you, Father. Keep me safe in your arms. I have been writing in this God journal for two years now.

IV
A FINAL WORD

Saturday, September 1, 2018

This book has covered my path from Buddhism, through the darkness of divorce, to a renewed walk with the God of my youth. Interwoven with this spiritual journey is the path of a Vietnam veteran who suffered from PTSD, mental illness, insanity and chronic alcoholism who ultimately found recovery and redemption.

I have spent the past eighteen years walking with the Lord. He has helped me through the good and the bad times. My life has new meaning and purpose. This once broken vessel is now being used to honor Him!

In 2010, we joined a country gospel music group and started ministering for God through song and testimony. Our theme song was, "I Saw the Light." We ministered to people who were struggling with drug and alcohol addiction. We ministered to them on the streets, in rehab, and in homeless shelters. We brought them a message of hope. If God could change our circumstances – if he could change us – then he could change them too.

May 15, 2011, I was baptized in the Holy Spirit at an Assemblies of God church service. Now we were called and sent out by the Holy Spirit to share Jesus. For the next two years, we stayed busy working for the Lord. Then on July 25, 2013, I was prayed for, washed in the blood of Jesus and the stronghold of PTSD removed sufficiently that I was able to work with fellow veterans. In May 2014, Lori retired from her job so we could spend all of our time working for Jesus. In October, we sold our house, downsized to a townhouse, and began to travel and minister. Life could not get much better than this.

However, God had more changes in store for us. On Memorial Day weekend in 2014, a friend told me about Dave Roever, a fellow Vietnam veteran, and a well-known evangelist, who was going to be speaking at a church in the area. Dave had been burned over fifty percent of his body by a phosphorus grenade in Vietnam. A Viet Cong sniper shot the grenade as he was getting ready to throw it on to a riverbank.

Lori and I went and listened to Dave at the church. When he spoke, he did not focus on the combat trauma. Instead, he talked about God, family, and country. He said something that forever changed the way I would look at ministry. He said, "If you don't have anything worth dying for, then maybe you don't have anything worth living for." I felt like he was looking right at me. Then he said, "I was willing to die for my country, and you can see that I almost did." "I am still willing to die for my family and Jesus." "What are you willing to die for?" What was I willing to die for! I rushed to speak with him after the service. We talked about his ministry work in Vietnam. I told him that I could still speak Vietnamese. He encouraged me to call and talk with the man in his Texas office that was in charge of his Vietnam ministry.

The following week I called and spoke with Pastor Dan Dang. He told me about all the work Roever Educational Assistance Program (REAP) International was doing in Vietnam. In October 2014, I traveled to Texas where I met with Pastor Dan and attended the REAP International Vietnamese pastors conference. Pastor Dan asked me to give my testimony to the Vietnamese pastors at the conference. Then he added, "…do it in Vietnamese." It had been a long time since I tried to tell my story in Vietnamese. I was amazed at how the Vietnamese words flowed out of me. That weekend I saw my life go full circle. God showed me how my testimony, from Buddhist to Christian, would be used for His Glory! I was one hundred percent sold-out to this new calling in my life. Another door had been opened, and we began stepping out in ministry to the Vietnamese people

In March 2015, Lori and I went to Vietnam with Pastor Dan's ministry team and a group of Vietnam veterans. I had not been back to Vietnam since 1998. I was concerned about going back after nearly dying on that trip. A veteran friend was very encouraging. He thought I should go back. He told me, "You went to Vietnam in the 60's to kill, you returned in the 90's to die, now you are going back to heal." What he said really made sense to me. Not only could I heal, but also my testimony of what Jesus did in my life might help others find healing. We had an amazing time on the trip praising the Lord and ministering to the veterans who accompanied us, and the Vietnamese people.

In April of 2016, we were asked to join Dave Roever's staff and told we would be working for Pastor Dan and REAP International. We moved to Fort Worth and worked in their headquarters for the next year. At this same time, I was given the opportunity to become an associate pastor at Pastor Dan's Vietnamese church. I had been credentialed in 2015 as a minister by the Assemblies of God church. Today we continue to travel to Vietnam with the REAP mission team. Lori and I feel a special connection with the Vietnamese people in this country and look forward to our mission trips to Vietnam.

That brings us to this day and what a beautiful day it is. Lori and I have eighteen years of walking with the Lord and eighteen years of sobriety. We are living a life of God's unmerited grace and mercy. We have never been happier in our marriage. Lori is the love of my life. She is God's gift to me and is one of the most spiritual people that I have ever known. We have a blessed life together and walk hand-in-hand on the road to recovery. We are thankful to God and our AA program for this new way of life. Thank you, Jesus!

In AA they have a saying that, "God doesn't close one door without opening up a better one." This has been so true in my life. Although I often stumbled, God has always been with me. He has never left me. He has always had a plan for my life. I frequently tell people, "God can take everything that has happened in your life. The good, the bad, and the ugly and use it for his glory." Finally, I now know that from a life of shattered dreams and broken promises, we can come up out of the darkest abyss and shine for Jesus! We are free at last!

ABOUT THE CO-AUTHOR
STAN CORVIN, JR.

Born in a small town in West Texas in 1944, Stan grew up in a military family. His father was a career USAF fighter pilot retiring as a colonel. His mother was an elementary school teacher frequently teaching on air force bases where they lived.

After attending Texas Tech University for his undergraduate studies, Stan was drafted into the US Army. While in basic training, he was accepted into the Army's helicopter flight school, graduating nine months later in December 1967. Serving in the US Army from 1967 to 1974, he flew combat helicopter missions in Vietnam in 1968-69 and for the CIA in 1971-72 attaining the rank of captain. Stan resigned his commission in 1974 to pursue a career in banking.

In 2014, after forty years in banking, Stan retired, and in 2015 wrote, and published *Vietnam Saga: Exploits of a Combat Helicopter Pilot,* a personal memoir about his flying experiences during the war. (The second edition was published in 2017.) The book includes the story of Stan's being shot down twice in ten minutes trying to save a downed US Air Force fighter pilot who was surrounded by 12,500 North Vietnamese Army soldiers at Khe Sanh in the Ashau valley. After crawling out of the second burning helicopter with his back broken, Stan was shot in the chest and stomach five times by an AK-47. Thirteen hours later, he and the other helicopter crewmembers were finally rescued.

In 2017 Stan co-authored and published *Jet Pioneer: A Fighter Pilot's Memoir*, which is the amazing autobiography of Major General Carl G. Schneider, USAF (Ret.) One of only six men to ever enter the military as an enlisted private, he rose through the ranks to become a two-star general flying jet aircraft in the Korean War and in Vietnam.

In 2018, Stan wrote and published *Echoes of the Hunt*. Taking place in West Texas, the book is a true story of his ten-day stalking of a trophy mule deer. While sitting alone beside a warm fireplace and in a cold deer stand, he recalls childhood stories of hunting adventures with his father, grandfather, and uncles.

Stan is the president and founder of Southwestern Legacy Press, LLC which is the publisher of the above books as well as *Vietnam Abyss: A Journal of Unmerited Grace*. All of these books are available for purchase through Amazon books, Kindle˚, Barnes & Noble˚ and as audiobooks through Audible.com˚ and iTunes˚.

Stan and his wife live in Fort Worth, Texas, and have a large family of seven grown children and fifteen grandchildren. As a long-time member of Alcoholics Anonymous, he has been soberly living happy, joyous and free for the last thirty-two years and looks forward to what God has in store for him in the future – one day at a time.

CPSIA information can be obtained
at www.ICGtesting.com
Printed in the USA
FFHW02n1222230918
48544334-52435FF